The Rock-em, Sock-em, Travelin' Sideways Dirt Show:
A History of Robert Smawley's NDRA

by
Gary L. Parker

WALDENHOUSE PUBLISHERS, INC.
WALDEN, TENNESSEE

The Rock-em, Sock-em, Travelin' Sideways Dirt Show: A History of Robert Smawley's NDRA
Copyright © 2016 Gary L. Parker. All rights reserved. No part of this book may be reproduced in any form or by any electronic or mechanical means including information storage and retrieval systems, without permission in writing from the author. The only exception is by a reviewer, who may quote short excerpts in a review.
Front cover art by Kent Harrelson.
Type and design by Karen Paul Stone
ISBN: 978-1-935186-69-4
Library of Congress Control Number: 2016900468
   SPO028000 Sports & Recreation - Motor Sports
   SPO019000 Sports & Recreation - History
   TRA001050 Transportation: Automotive - History
   HIS036120 History: United States - South
Waldenhouse Publishers, Inc.
100 Clegg Street, Signal Mountain, Tennessee 37377 USA
888-222-8228 • www.waldenhouse.com
Printed in the United States of America
Tells the story of the first national touring series for dirt late models. Robert Smawley, founder of the National Dirt Racing Association (NDRA) was a visionary promoter who was clearly years ahead of his time. He brought money and national fame to late model dirt racing and its drivers. His series changed the sport of dirt racing forever. All of today's national touring series owe their beginnings to Smawley and his "travelin' dirt show." 164 photographs -- Provided by Publisher

Other books by this author:
Red Clay and Dust: The Evolution of Southern Dirt Racing
Copyright 2015 © Gary L. Parker ISBN: 978-1-935186-61-8
Library of Congress Control Number: 2015911265
To order contact the author, Gary L. Parker
1517 Maxwell Road, Chattanooga, TN 37412
423-580-2690 • eparker0923@gmail.com
                or go to
www. waldenhouse.com – or – www.amazon.com

Table of Contents

Foreword by Rodney Combs — v

Thoughts on the NDRA by Bob Markos — ix

Acknowledgments — xiii

Introduction — xv

Chapter One: Robert Wayne Smawley: Life Before The NDRA — 19

Chapter Two: Smawley's Traveling Dirt Series: Would It Work? — 31

Chapter Three: At Long Last The Series Begins-The First Season — 40

Chapter Four: The NDRA Series Points Champions — 58

Chapter Five: Rising Stars On The NDRA Tour — 89

Chapter Six: The National Dirt Racing Association's Tour Busters — 101

Chapter Seven: Robert Being Robert — 117

Chapter Eight: Some Milestone Races Of The NDRA — 129

Chapter Nine: Reasons Behind The Sudden Demise Of The NDRA — 146

Chapter Ten: The End Of A Dream: Why Robert Pulled The Plug — 156

More Photos from the Rock-em, Sock-em, Travelin' Sideways Dirt Show — 159

Order blank for more copies of books by Gary Parker — 185

The Rock-em, Sock-em, Travelin' Sideways Dirt Show

Robert Smawley with his famous checkered flag vest. Photo by David Chobat.

Gary L. Parker

Foreword

Rodney Combs
National Dirt Late Model Hall of Famer

When Robert Smawley came up with the NDRA, at that point in time we were, meaning myself, running one-hundred, two-hundred lap or more pavement races for just a few thousand dollars at places like Indianapolis Raceway Park, Winchester, Indiana and Dayton and Cincinnati, Ohio. So when we heard about NDRA having an event in Tennessee that was paying ten thousand dollars to win, well it was pretty simple to figure out for myself what to do, 'cause I had run dirt in the past and when you see something like that you say to yourself, hey, let's try this!

When we went down to see what it was all about, it was pretty damn professional, and what was said was no bull. It happened, and everything that followed it. Robert was an innovator, a hell of a showman, and a promoter all wrapped into one. He was definitely the "Elvis Presley of Dirt Stock Car Racing" – just the way he dressed, the things he came up with, and for what he was able to accomplish in the sport. He put together one heck of a sponsor package and eventually a program where ten or twelve of us became what you would call the early traveling outlaw gang – sorta like the "Dirty Dozen" that came about later.

He knew how to promote and make it work. He was just a different breed never seen before in short track racing.

Yeah sure, there was the ASA (American Speed Association) at that time, but that was more of a regional type deal for asphalt. But on dirt, NDRA, with its national flavor and big time payoffs was just unheard of and way ahead of its time.

At about that time Larry [Moore] and I weren't doing much dirt stuff, as we were back running around on pavement. Yet Robert, the promo man that he was, came up to Ohio to visit with us to get us to come down and run his series. And for us, we never really had the opportunity to compete for that kind of money before – it was new to us. He also offered to take care of us pretty well and it was like, wow, this is pretty cool, 'cause we were gonna be traveling and getting paid such good money for it, so I said, "Count me in!"

So for a while there we were headed south, much more than north in a way. We got to race a lot of new venues that we had never been to before and on top of it get paid well. Again, very cool! Eventually when we all raced together as a group with NDRA, it was just such an extremely talented bunch running one-hundred lap races, and by the end of the night you wouldn't even find a black mark on your car. That's just how good those guys were. Nobody ever ran over anybody, and to run with them and not have your car beat up was pretty damn neat. It definitely produced some of the best dirt shows ever run, period. We traveled and went down the road together, stayed at motels together, hung out by the pool, the whole deal, and when we raced together it was good clean competition.

It's also amazing the sponsorships and the money we got – I mean guys who came along, we got a thousand dollars to go to them shows back then against what we won. And here we were in pick-ups, ramp trucks, nothing fancy at all, and we're at Muskogee, Oklahoma, or Chicago and getting paid well to do our thing. Robert definitely had the NASCAR of dirt back then, and we'd go on the radio and go to dealerships and do things to promote the shows and he'd take care of us.

Basically when we started there with NDRA you only had Jig-A-Lo and Roscoe Smith building race cars for dirt. NDRA pretty much started the evolution of the store bought racer, with Ed Howe, who primarily built cars for asphalt, getting onboard and putting together a dirt program for me. Then all of a sudden here comes C.J. Rayburn, Bullitt, Barry Wright and a bunch more including Mark [Richards] and myself getting started at WRC. Just that quick things took off as race cars began being built by a number of different designers specifically for dirt.

To win you had to have the light weight stuff with plenty of flexibility as long as it stayed within the lines of safety. It was pretty much the beginning of the "keeping up with the Joneses theory".

NDRA took me to a whole new level, as it not only let me race for a living, but then helped put my car building business on the map in selling chassis all around the country, along with Australia, Mexico and Canada. Each of us also got plenty of big time national exposure. Even NASCAR knew about us and how tough the racing was. NDRA meant a lot to me in that regard – how I got to do it, how it got my business started and what it led me to down the road.

It led me to NASCAR stuff with Jim Stacy first as my sponsor and then being able to race his NASCAR cars. So much NDRA did for my life and my career, that's the truth; it's not made up. It put the decals on my car, got me the sponsors and brought professionalism to us and the sport. We were one of the first to have crew uniforms, painted up all our equipment, always kept things clean, just anything to help make this thing work, which it did.

We had some great runs and wins with NDRA such as being with Ed [Howe] and being so fast, lapping the field at Brunswick, Georgia or so many times running one – two with Larry – that was cool stuff. Also at Granite City racing together with Larry and Kevin Gundaker and running away, sorta off into the sunset, and doing it so easily. That's where writer Joyce Standridge from *Stock Car Racing Magazine* labeled me with the "Superman" thing, which brought us more exposure that turned into some great extra P.R. for myself.

Yet there were some issues. In 1982 we could have won the NDRA championship, but there was some shenanigans going on, and Robert and I had a falling out. So with two races to go for the season I told him, "Ya know you could just take this thing and stick it you know where." I probably could have won it anyway, but I was pissed and I just didn't run those last two shows and gave it away.

Robert didn't think I was serious but believe me I was. I've always raced fair, and it took a lot out of me as it really shouldn't have ever happened, but it did. The next year we went back to the series thinking we'll show him what we're made of, and we won the championship, which was very satisfying.

Everybody knew Robert was a party animal. He loved every part of it – the fans, his women, the pig roasts after the races, the whole thing. That was his gig – his persona. Yet, in the end it was probably his undoing. We had to boycott him, because it got to where he was more worried about his girls and the partying than his drivers and his races. So we got together as a group, eight of us or so, 'cause we had to show him things had to change – had to prove a point, and we did.

Many will tell you Robert's drinking, his girls and all that stuff let him get in trouble with his sponsors and led to NDRA's ultimate demise. It's such a shame though, how he just let something so good just slip away. Whatever the deal was, some might not understand this, but in my case I'd have to thank the man for what he did. No question about it, what we got to do, race for a living at that time and turn dirt late model racing into a business was all because of Robert Smawley. He was a unique individual who did things nobody else had ever done, and he was very sharp at how to put things together and put on a show.

It was a very special time in racing and I am certainly glad I was a part of it.

Rodney Combs

Gary L. Parker

Thoughts on the NDRA

Bob Markos
National Racing Historian/Writer

Having been frozen in a chunk of ice for the past thirty years I remember all too well those almost mythical exploits of Bobby Smawley, the National Dirt Racing Association and his entourage of legendary mudslingers as if it were just yesterday.

I'm speaking about Robert Smawley and his organization named the NDRA, which propelled dirt track stock car racing from the backwoods as we knew it into the ranks of professionalism. Smawley and his magical group revolutionized the sport as in just what seemed a snap of the fingers, dirt late model racing took on an almost fairy-tale type persona that evolved itself from a rustic grassroots pastime into a national phenomenon. NDRA's niche carved in history served as a memorable era considered by many as the "Golden Age of Dirt Late Model Racing."

There was a time when hundreds, maybe thousands of dirt stock car racers roamed the lower forty-eight aimlessly searching for identity, as well as enough jack to sustain their weekend habits and operations. Bonanza type, big paying shows were few and far between and disappointment and despair was prevalent across the Dirt Late Model community.

Yet in the late 1970's, a man by the name of Robert Smawley saw this ripe plum to be picked, and formed the National Dirt Racing Association, enticing this throng of dirt racing drifters by offering them jaw dropping, never before seen paydays. Overnight the press, the fans and of course the participants themselves flocked to these events like pilgrims to the Promised Land. With the scrumptious payola, the mammoth fields of contestants and the hoopla of Smawley's snazzy spectacles all wrapped together in one neat package, Dirt Late Models quickly found themselves soaring from the back pages in the trades to the national headlines.

Smawley, a former motorcycle racer turned Kingsport area businessman, rose up from the mountains of Tennessee like a phoenix to become the redeemer of Dirt Stock Car Racing, promising fame and fortune to all those who would climb aboard - so many of us became followers and believers. He had set the standard in the sport, gathering together America's top dawgs on dirt, selling his notion of a traveling circuit to a national racing audience. For so long it was the baddest gig around.

No doubt Smawley was a marketing master and the ultimate public relations wiz, landing big name beer and tobacco sponsorships while transforming weekend dirt track racing warriors such as Larry Moore, Buck Simmons, Rodney Combs, Mike Duvall, Jerry Inmon, and Jeff Purvis into national traveling cult like heroes.

He once proudly boasted, "I am the NASCAR of Dirt", although the flamboyant Smawley had darn good reason, for at one time his NDRA stood in line behind NASCAR and Indy Car Racing as the most popular motorsport in the nation. His NDRA constituents called it by far the best thing that ever happened to dirt racing. By establishing himself as an aggressive free thinking visionary, Smawley became the toast of the town. Some believed he could change the course of mighty rivers, bend steel in his bare hands and that he stood for truth, justice and the American Late Model way. There were others though who would express the absolute opposite, saying he was nothing more than a charlatan and a rogue.

From its magnificent debut in August of 1978 to its final performance in November of 1985, Smawley's NDRA rode a rollercoaster of emotions. Eventually, promises were not met and things began to unravel as there were short fields of cars, contractual differences, canceled dates and bonuses, and a points fund not delivered. In the spring of 1986, a letter was sent out from the NDRA offices claiming that, due to insurance reasons, the 1986 season was a wash and thus came the end of NDRA. Along with it went the point fund monies from the completed 1985 campaign, which was to be presented at the season's first event.

But, what on earth could have happened to allow Smawley's remarkable Rock-em Sock-em Dirt Show to derail? Only Robert himself or those extremely close to him would be able to reveal the true story.

Following NDRA's folding, Smawley left the scene just as quickly as he had arrived to live in seclusion the rest of his days. He passed away in October of 1998 at age 53 from leukemia.

Hall of Famer Larry Moore once confided to me that Robert and the NDRA were the greatest combination in the history of the sport. But, as we continued our conversation, he began to paint another picture – one that hinted at mistrust and frustration. Enough so that Moore, whose name has been synonymous with the group's illustrious history, eventually abandoned ship himself, to seek fortune with other organizations of that period formed primarily to compete directly head on with Smawley.

Down the road the magic continued to disperse as aside from Moore, other headlining loyalists pulled up stakes to earn a living on dirt ovals elsewhere. Those close to Smawley revealed that he had actually become frustrated with the whole thing. His goal was to organize Late Model racing from coast to coast and when other groups began to form during this period and some of his long-time followers deserted, he just couldn't understand. He thought he was giving his all, and now they and others were turning their backs on him and the sport.

There were also some competitors who refused to wear NDRA sponsorship insignia, citing religious or anti-alcohol and tobacco beliefs – Smawley would only cringe, accusing those who would take such a stand as being non-supporters of auto racing as a whole.

But like any story there are additional motives. Robert tired of trying to convert his driver's images from a scrappy rag-tag group of traveling outlaws (which he originally prescribed for them) into modern day sophisticated press-worthy racers. Others in the know also hinted of deteriorating fitness issues, as at only 39 years of age Smawley's wild and exorbitant lifestyle combined with daily business pressures led to his failing health.

Though in the end, failure usually always comes down to economics. Due to contractual differences with NDRA's final corporate benefactor, the Stroh's Beer Corporation, Smawley would find himself incapable of fulfilling his obligations and continue on with his vehicle. Thus the final curtain had fallen upon the sport's first prominent national dirt racing series. Of course non-payment of the 1985 season points fund was a tad bit more than just a dose of sour grapes – those who traveled, participated and gave their all were extremely vocal. They felt they had been hoodwinked, basically cheated blind, and allegations of litigation began to surface.

It was a sad ending to such a celebrated movement, so many years ahead of its time.

So was Robert Smawley, the man who claimed he hated a liar, but loved a bullshitter, the greatest promo man the sport has ever known or something completely different? I guess it depends on whose opinion you care to consider, as there were many from both sides of the catch fence who witnessed it all. In any case, Robert left an indelible mark on the Dirt Late Model scene. During its existence NDRA was one of the greatest and most talked about dirt stock car organizations to ever grace this planet. And even through all the bad times Smawley was still able to make dreams come true.

Like no one before him, he took generations of red-blooded American dirt racers, organized them and made them national heroes, offering them a way to make a living doing what they loved most. He brought aboard Corporate America, something that is still somewhat deficient in the sport even to this day. He presented showmanship to the sport like no other before and no one has ever since. He introduced with regularity the big-dollar show and raised the bar, forcing promoters everywhere to offer more money to those men who built their own equipment and raced like it was religion. In addition, car builders evolved during this era and began constructing real race cars, so many developed extremely safer than in the past, for these men to chase those lofty paychecks.

In 2001, Robert Smawley was inducted into the National Dirt Late Model Hall of Fame's great inaugural class. In my opinion, like any true historical journalist has been instructed – through time when the legend becomes fact…print the legend.

Bob Markos

Gary L. Parker

Acknowledgments

This book on the history of Robert Smawley's, National Dirt Racing Association (NDRA) could not have been written without the help of a number of great and wonderful individuals. First, I want to think Eva Taylor Hunter, Michael "Cotton" Duke, Buddy Duke, and Connie Noel Melton for providing me with preliminary information and introducing me to other key people who played an important role in Smawley's life and his series.

One of those people I was introduced to was Robert's daughter, Chelsea Smawley Martino, who was kind enough to give me permission to use all of her dad's private photo albums. Through the use of these private photos, I was able to tell a much better story of the NDRA's colorful history. Again, thank you Chelsea. Also, as promised, I used your favorite photo on the back cover.

Two other people also played a very important role in this book. First, I want to thank the national racing historian and writer, Bob Markos. This man is a walking encyclopedia of racing knowledge. His help was key to the writing of this book, providing important photos, race posters, and other little know insights into Smawley's series. Also, a special thanks to him for his "Thoughts on the NDRA." I proudly include Bob's section in the book. Finally, Rodney Combs is owed a very special thanks for writing the foreword to this book. He was one of the most influential drivers of the NDRA series, and the foreword along with his other contributions help make this a better story of Smawley's ground breaking NDRA national touring series.

The background cover photo came from Smawley's private collection and is the photo used on the cover of the 1979 NDRA yearbook. We tried to find the person responsible for taking such a great photo, but in the end had no success. I told Kent Harrelson, the designer of the cover, "We could have looked at a million photos and would have never found a better photo for the cover of this book." It is a great photo and we take no credit for this beautiful picture of late model dirt racing. Thank you Kent for another fine cover.

There are many other people I wish to take this time to thank. They include Jo Zimmerman, Fred Vineyard, his sister Betty Vineyard-Price and her late husband, Darwin "Shon" Price. Also, David "Peanut" Jenkins, Doug Sopha, H.C. "Fuzzy" Orange, Johnny Robinson, Mickey Swims, Jeff Smith, Leon Archer, Larry Moore, Jeff Purvis, Mike Duvall, and many many others. You know who you are, and if I failed to mention you, I sincerely thank you also.

Finally, thanks to Robert Wayne Smawley for being the visionary dirt late model promoter who brought dirt late model racing to the national scene, and along the way changed the sport of dirt racing forever. He was a showman and visionary promoter who was truly ahead of his time. "The Rock-em, Sock-em, Travelin' Sideways Dirt Show" is truly the best description of his NDRA.

Gary L. Parker

Introduction

After completing the book, RED CLAY AND DUST, I was looking through the manuscript one day, and the section in chapter three on the NDRA caught my attention. The series had such a profound impact on the future of late model dirt racing, I decided the series was worthy of an entire book devoted to it.

The National Dirt Racing Association (NDRA) was the country's first national touring series for dirt late models. It was the visionary creation of Kingsport, Tennessee's Robert Smawley, its organizer, promoter, and president. The NDRA was Robert Smawley's "Rock-Em, Sock-Em, Travelin' Sideways Dirt Show." In its almost eight years of existence, the series would go on to change the sport of late model dirt racing forever.

During its relatively short history, 1978 to 1985, the series introduced a number of changes to late model racing. Some provided positive results for the sport. For example, it made regional drivers into national dirt stars. A set of uniform rules was introduced for the race cars, including a standardized weight limit for race cars. Also, corporate sponsors such as, Dodge, Chrysler, Stroh's Beer, Schlitz Beer, and Consolidated Cigar ushered in the era of large purses for late model dirt series racing. However, it took the unfortunate death of racing star Jim Dunn, at an NDRA race in Paducah, Kentucky in 1983, to force the elimination of the electronic fuel pump and usher in the standardization of fuel-cell specifications. On the negative side, it spelled the doom of the "home built" race car, causing a racing chassis war. The series also increased racing costs on such things as engines, and the manufactured racing chassis, forcing a number of race teams out of the sport.

At the time, the NDRA became the "major league" of late model dirt racing, setting the standard for many of today's national dirt late model tours, like the Lucas Oil Late Model Dirt Series, and the World of Outlaws Late Model Series.

In the pages ahead we will take a look at Robert Smawley's national dirt late model tour, examining some of the reasons why he started the series, the ways in which he organized it, how he brought the drivers, promoters, and track owners on board, and finally, the way he convinced the sponsors to provide the money and products necessary to run a national racing series.

Then our focus shifts to the NDRA Points Champions and the path each took to the series title. Also, we take a look at some of the "rising stars" of the series and how their racing careers have gone since the tour ended. Next, we profile a few of the "tour busters" of the series – those local drivers that were able to score a major win over Smawley's regular touring drivers.

The book would not be complete without a chapter on "Robert Being Robert," showing his funny side and how he sometimes used it to his advantage on just about everyone around him, from his staff, to the drivers, the car owners, track owners, promoters, and even the series' sponsors. Then some of the milestone races that took place during the series will be profiled, unique races such as "The Super Bowl of Dirt," held inside the Pontiac Silverdome. Also, many of the big money races that took place during the series' almost eight year run will be examined.

Finally, we take a look at some of the reasons for the sudden demise of Smawley's National Dirt Racing Association, taking a close look at some of the things that could have caused the abrupt end to the nation's first national late model tour. According to many who knew him, when Smawley started the NDRA he truly believed in his heart he could create a dirt late model version of NASCAR's cup series. As you will see after reading this book, he came "Damn Close."

Gary L. Parker

Eva Taylor, the First Miss NDRA. Photo by David Chobat.

The Rock-em, Sock-em, Travelin' Sideways Dirt Show

Jo Zimmerman, Miss NDRA. Photo by David Chobat.

Gary L. Parker

Chapter One

Robert Wayne Smawley: Life Before the NDRA

This chapter takes a look at Robert Smawley's early life in his hometown of Kingsport, Tennessee, examining some of his interests while growing up. Attention then shifts to Robert's love of motorcycles and his professional motorcycle career, first as a teenager, and then as a young adult. Also, Smawley's many business interests in his hometown will be mentioned. We then take a look at his career promoting motorcycle races, a few rock band concerts, and other promotional ventures. Finally, we look at Smawley, the visionary, the promoter, and the showman. In the end we see him as a business promoter who was clearly years ahead of his time.

Robert Wayne Smawley was born on February 17, 1945, in the Northeastern Tennessee town of Kingsport. He was the only child of Robert Earl, and Dorothy Hall Smawley. Robert's Parents were a hardworking couple who lived on, oddly enough, Dorothy Street while young Robert was growing up. His mother, Dorothy, was a professional nurse for seventeen years; while his father, Robert Earl, a military veteran, worked at the Kingsport Press for many years. While growing up Robert and his father enjoyed hunting and fishing together. Robert had a very close relationship with both his parents. His parents would later help Robert with a number of his

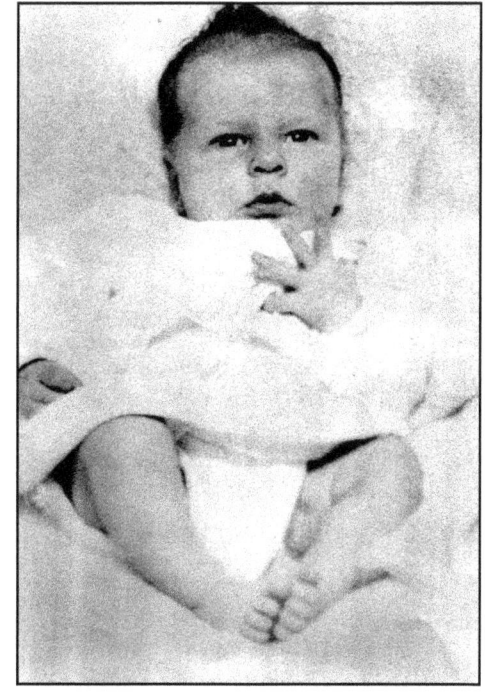

Photo of one month old Robert Smawley taken in 1945. Photo from the Robert Smawley Collection.

A young Robert Smawly at one of his early promotions. Photo from the Robert Smawley Collection.

Robert's mother, Dorothy Hall Smawley. Photo from the Robert Smawley Collection.

Robert's father, Robert Earl. Photo from the Robert Smawley Collection.

business ventures, including a liquor store and rental property. After Robert's dad died during his teen years, he maintained a very close relationship with his mother throughout his life. Robert once said in a family album, "Through my life as being her son, her beliefs have guided me into manhood, and her moral and financial support of my ideas have brought success into my life."

Dorothy Smawley, like Robert's father, was well liked in the Kingsport Community. According to long time friend and future NDRA employee, Michael "Cotton" Duke, "Dorothy was the one the neighbors went to when there was a problem in the area." Duke went on to say, "In most cases, she took care of whatever was going on. She was one of a kind, and everyone liked the way she watched over her community." He closed by saying with a big "Cotton Duke" smile, "Dorothy watched over and took a keen interest in her Dorothy Street. She was almost like a 'den mother' to Robert and his friends."

Robert and his mother. They had a very close relationship throughout Robert's life. Photo provided by Buddy Duke.

As far as schooling went, young Smawley attended elementary school at Washington Elementary, went to middle school at John Sevier Middle, and for a few years was a student at Dobbins-Bennett High School. Robert never finished high school; however he was a very smart young man with business head on his shoulders at a very young age. According to many who knew him, "Robert was always thinking of new ways to make a dollar." He spent his teenage years with a number of friends that included Michael and Buddy Duke, Tim Taylor, and perhaps one of his best friends while growing up, Johnny Robinson.

Robinson told me in a recent interview, "Robert was always playing jokes on people, and getting a lot of us in trouble." He then said, "Somehow Robert was good at getting me and a lot of others in trouble; however that little devil had a way of always keeping himself out of the trouble he created."

"Cotton" Duke once told me a funny trick Robert pulled on a friend. As we will discuss shortly, Robert loved to ride motorcycles. Cotton said, "Robert and a friend were riding motorcycles one day

Robert's long time girl friend, Jo Zimmerman. Photo from the Robert Smawley Collection.

in an upscale neighborhood in Kingsport." Duke continued, "As they were riding by some very large and expensive homes, Robert stopped in front of one of the houses and said he had left his helmet at a relative's house on a table at the top of the stairs. He asked the friend

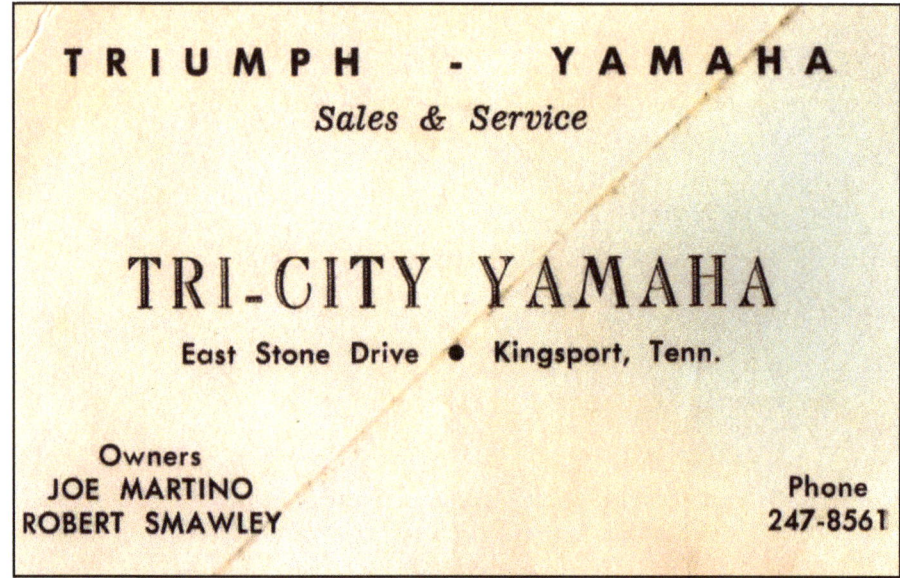

Business card from the Tri-City Yamaha shop owned by Robert Smawley and Joe Martino. Photo provided by Jo Zimmerman.

to run in and get the helmet for him." Cotton laughed at what happened next. He said, "That poor friend burst in running up the stairs to retrieve the helmet, only to find out from the homeowner, no one knew Robert and there was no helmet." Duke closed by saying with a big laugh, "As the red-faced friend came out of the house, Robert was howling with laughter." According to about everyone who knew him, "Robert was very good at playing practical jokes on about everyone he was around." We will see a lot of these antics later in the NDRA series; as it was just "Robert being Robert."

On several occasions, Robert's dad helped fund his son in a number of business ventures. Probably the most successful of these, according to long time girlfriend, Jo Zimmerman, was the Tri-City Yamaha Motorcycle Shop Smawley and Joe Martino opened on East Stone Drive in Kingsport. Robert was an avid fan of the motorcycle, both for pleasure, and later as a pretty good racer himself. Zimmerman said, "The shop started out with the Yamaha dealership, but later added Kawasaki, and a number of other cycle brands."

This was the start of two important developments in Robert's life: motorcycle racing at the novice and professional level, and later

Young Robert in front of motorcycle shop in Kingsport, TN. Photo from the Robert Smawley Collection.

Smawley taking a break during one of his professional motorcycle races. Photo from the Robert Smawley Collection.

the start of his career as a professional promoter. Other than promoting a few rock band concerts (which turned out to be a disaster), one of Smawley's first successful ventures as a promoter was promoting AMA sanctioned motorcycle races at the old Appalachian Speedway, located off highway 11, in his hometown of Kingsport in the early 1970's. One of the early races he promoted was the AMA sanctioned "Southeastern Classic Motorcycle Race" at the Appalachian Speedway in April of 1972.

In true Smawley form, Robert had to plan, organize, promote, and run the motorcycle event. At this event, we see the early beginnings of his visionary skills. Smawley not only had to reassure the community that what was taking place was a professional motorcycle race, and not 15,000 "Hell's Angels" roaring into Kingsport. He also had to ready the track for the crowd by enlarging the parking facilities, along with adding a large number of additional seats for the expected

Promotional ad for the Southeastern Classic Motorcycle Race held at the Appalachian Speedway. Ad provided by Jo Zimmerman.

The Rock-em, Sock-em, Travelin' Sideways Dirt Show

An ad for a motorcycle race Robert promoted at Cleveland, TN. Ad from the Robert Smawley Collection.

overflow crowd. Robert came through in style, pulling the event off with one of his classic promotional trademarks, "The biggest race and largest purse for an event." The Southeastern Classic Motorcycle Race had one of the largest crowds for an AMA Classic event ever in the South. The event also had a $9,700 purse, which was the largest ever for a Classic event. This was an early example of "Vintage Robert," the visionary, showman and promoter all rolled into one.

Robert went on to promote several other motorcycle events, including races in Cleveland, Tennessee, at the Motorcycle Raceway (at the Cleveland Fairgrounds), and a couple of Daytona events. However, in another of his visionary motorcycle promotions, Smawley saw the opportunity to enter the closed circuit television market in 1974. According to Buddy Duke, "Robert smelled the money he could make by getting the closed circuit rights to Evil Knievel's Snake River Canyon jump." Buddy said, "Ole Robert got ahead of everyone in the area and got the Evil Knievel rights in, not only the Tri-Cities market, but also I think he got the rights in, Ashville, Knoxville, Chattanooga, and even Roanoke, Virginia." So, on September 8, 1974, as the whole world watched dare devil Evil Knievel try and fail to jump the Snake River Canyon in Twin Falls, Idah, guess who had the foresight to have the closed circuit rights to the Knievel jump in most of East Tennessee and a lot of the surrounding areas. None other than Robert Smawley.

As mentioned earlier, Smawley was a pretty good motorcycle racer himself. He competed in several Novice, Amateur, Junior Dirt, and Pro races in Tennessee, North Carolina, and other areas. He even ran a couple of the big Daytona AMA races finishing in the top 20.

Later, Robert would even try his hand at dirt track racing in a race car. However, his career in car racing was short lived as a racing accident ended that dream. It was during his short lived career with the dirt cars that Smawley saw the sad state of dirt racing throughout the South. He saw that the high costs involved with racing could never be made profitable because of the small purses the tracks were offering for their weekly shows ($500 to win was a big purse at the time). There was no cooperation at all between track owners and promoters; each track was isolated and working on their own. In addition, Robert saw the disorganization at most of the tracks he visited.

The Rock-em, Sock-em, Travelin' Sideways Dirt Show

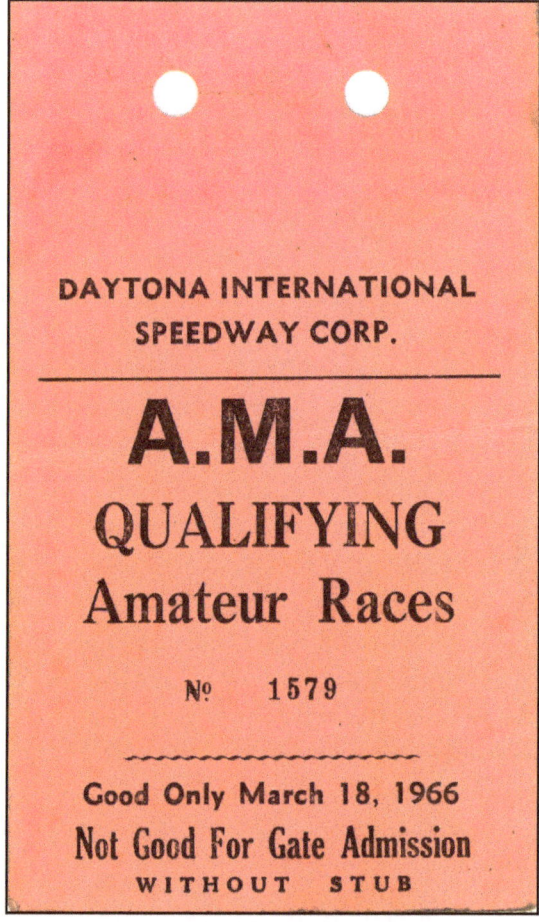

One of Robert's Qualifying passes for a race he competed in at Daytona in 1966. Pass from the Robert Smawley Collection.

This included no rules for either the cars or drivers. Also, a lot of the track owners and promoters would advertise a purse, then give excuses not to pay but part of what was advertised. In some cases the purses were not paid at all. He also saw that most tracks paid the top five most of the announced purse, while paying little or nothing to the remaining drivers. In a lot of cases, a number of drivers ended up with nothing, not even tow money. This got Smawley to thinking, and you know what happens when he starts thinking.

This thinking, planning, and promoting is what the remainder of this book is about. The visionary ideas of Robert Wayne Smawley, the man who organized, promoted, and started the first national touring series for dirt late models. The National Dirt Racing Association (NDRA) would change the face of late model dirt racing forever.

Chapter Two

Smawley's Traveling Dirt Show - Would It Work?

Kingsport, Tennessee, businessman Robert Smawley's National Dirt Racing Association (NDRA) just didn't happen overnight. Although the first "official" NDRA race, the "Valvoline 100," was not held until August 5, 1978 at East Alabama Motor Speedway in Phenix City, Alabama, the series was several years in the making. It had been talked about by Robert and others for a number of years. But in 1976, a Dahlonega, Georgia, dirt late model star by the name of Doug Kenimer became the "NDRA Ambassador" to late model dirt racing.

Doug Kenimer, the "NDRA Ambassador" to Smawley's series, was instrumental in helping organize the NDRA. Photo provided by Paul's Auto Parts.

In the mid-70's late model dirt racing was in trouble, not only in the South, but all over the country. The cost of racing had skyrocketed, while the racing purses had failed to keep pace with the expenses being incurred by the drivers and car owners. A driver was lucky if he found a track willing to pay $600 to win a race. Add to that the dishonesty of some track owners and promoters (not paying the announced purse, or not paying at all in some cases), and you had a situation that was likely to spell doom for late model dirt racing. Small purses, dishonest track owners and promoters were making it hard for the honest ones, along with the drivers, to survive.

So, in 1976 Doug Kenimer went on a traveling "racing vacation" throughout a large part of the country. He listened to what the drivers and car owners were saying about the poor state of the sport. Doug then brought back important data that would be instrumental to Smawley in organizing and making the NDRA a reality.

Robert at work in his office in Kingsport, organizing his NDRA series. Photo provided by Bobby Duke.

After much planning and organizing, Robert put together an NDRA Team that included: Robert Smawley, President; Vice President, Bill Dale; NDRA Assistant, Michael "Cotton" Duke; Personal Assistant/Secretary, Connie Noel; Scorekeepers, Chris and Brenda Boals; Chief Pit Steward, H.C. "Fuzzy" Orange; and Miss NDRA, Eva Taylor. Also on board were announcer, Bob Harmon, and flagman, Bob Cooper. Later, Robert had a number of flagmans during the series. I had the pleasure of meeting another of them at the 2015 Dirt Track World Championship at Portsmouth, Ohio. Bob Smith is now a flagman at Portsmouth Raceway Park. Smith said he started flagging races for Robert, beginning with the World's Fair 100, that was held at Smoky Mountain Speedway in 1982.

With his team now in place, Smawley decided to have a couple of "Test Races" to be sure his racing series would run smoothly and successfully. At the Newport Speedway, in the nearby town of Newport, Tennessee, Robert scheduled the first of his "Test Races, " The

Gary L. Parker

Part of Smawley's NDRA team. Photo from NDRA program in 1979.

Southeastern Classic Dirt Championship. In June of 1978, he scheduled a $22,000 race, with an unheard of $10,000 going to the winner of the 100 lap late model event. The response was an overflow crowd of race fans and a pit filled with late model drivers from all over the

The NDRA announcer, the legendary Bob Harmon. Photo from the Robert Smawley collection.

country. One of the top dirt late model drivers in the South, Baldwin Georgia's Buck Simmons, won the action packed event that day.

In July of '78, Smawley was back at the Newport Speedway for his second and last, "Test Race." Again, an overflow crowd of excited race fans and talented late model drivers showed up for the race. This time the driver who had been a driving force in the development of the NDRA series, Doug Kenimer, won the $30,000 event, taking the $10,000 winner's share back to Georgia. After these two races, that Robert called "The Big Events," he was a believer in his series. He used his valuable motorcycle experience, both as a racer and a promoter, to help in organizing his new dirt late model series.

Among the things he proposed for his new, "Traveling Dirt Show," series included: paying, until now, the unheard of, $10,000 for winning one of his 100 lap events. In a recent interview, Buddy Duke, one of Robert's close friends said, "Robert didn't like the way most local tracks paid their racing purses." Buddy went on to say, "Robert called them 'Dolly Parton Purses,' because they were heavy at the top and paid the drivers at the bottom almost nothing." Finally, Duke said,

Bob Cooper, the flagman for the NDRA. Photo from the Robert Smawley collection.

The Rock-em, Sock-em, Travelin' Sideways Dirt Show

Program from the first "test race" held on June 9 and 10, 1978. Program provided by Jo Zimmerman.

"Robert wanted every driver in the race to receive a little money for their efforts. That's why he sometimes paid as much as $200 for finishing 24th." In addition, an NDRA race schedule was implemented: five more races for '78, and a race schedule for the '79 season. Also, a driver's point fund was organized and set up. And finally, series rules for both drivers and cars, were drawn up as a guideline at first. However, Smawley made it clear to the drivers and car owners that his NDRA rules would be enforced, starting with the 1979 season.

The last of '78 and through the '79 season saw most of the local tracks in the South suffering at the hands of the NDRA series. It seemed their weekly driver counts were down drastically, as most of the local stars were out chasing the big purses offered by Smawley. This caused many local tracks to decide either to join the NDRA tour, or to blacklist his dirt show and try to lure the local drivers back. The latter would not be necessary, because the NDRA established itself as the top level of dirt racing at the national level. Soon, many drivers realized they had neither the talent nor the money to chase Smawley's rainbow, with its pot of gold at the end.

The result of the high level of competition, and the money necessary to compete on the NDRA tour, saw the series find its own niche in the world of late model dirt racing. The series started having eagerly anticipated big events, scheduled far in advance, rather than the weekly shows that local tracks had enjoyed for years. After a couple of years of uncertainty between the local dirt tracks and Smawley's national series, both realized they had found their place in the dirt racing world. The weekly dirt track shows had their place in racing. They provided a proving ground for drivers who aspired to further their careers at the national level. In a sense, the NDRA became the "major league" of dirt racing. Robert sometimes envisioned his series becoming the dirt version of NASCAR's Cup Series. It was there for those drivers who had the talent to go to that next level.

Even today we see the same thing happening. One only has to look at the rising national stars like Jonathan Davenport, Chris Ferguson, Dennis Franklin, Casey Roberts, Josh Richards and Riley Hickman to name but a few, to see that only a few years ago they were the local stars racing the weekly shows at their favorite local track. Most of these drivers have gone on to race in the national tours like the Lucas Oil Late Model Dirt Series, the World of Outlaws Late Model Series, and even regional series like the Southern All Stars Racing Series. The NDRA was the first national touring series, and it changed the sport of late model dirt racing forever.

Photo showing the overflow crowd at Newport Speedway for the first "test race" in June of '78. Photo from the Robert Smawley collection.

This is the crowded pit area at Newport Speedway for the second "test race" in July of '78. Photo from the Robert Smawley collection.

One must keep in mind that Robert Smawley was like a trapeze artist operating without a safety net. He was back and forth with his ideas and plans for his new series. Robert had no "Safety Net" of data on previous touring series to fall back on. Reason being, there were no previous national dirt racing series' with which to make comparisons. Robert was on his own to live and die by the decisions he made. Perhaps one of his greatest attributes was his ability to quickly change something if it wasn't working. What made the NDRA a success was the visionary ideas Smawley continued to put in place throughout the series. He was simply a man who was just years ahead of his time.

The Rock-em, Sock-em, Travelin' Sideways Dirt Show

Chapter Three

At Long Last the Series Begins – The First Season

After many months of negotiations, media hype, test races, and fan and driver excitement, the Winter's Performance Pro-National Series (as the NDRA was known in the beginning) held it first "official" series race, the Valvoline 100, on August 5, 1978, at East Alabama Motor Speedway in Phenix City, Alabama. The first driver to see an NDRA checkered flag was a hometown late model driver by the name of Bobby Thomas, out dueling Kennesaw, Georgia's Charlie Mincey, who finished second.

That first season was late getting started in part because Smawley wanted to have two "test" races (held at the Newport (TN) Speedway), mentioned in an earlier chapter to get his new series organized; and to get a true gauge of driver and fan interest. As a result, he was able to schedule only five races in '78. So Robert extended the first season through the middle of the 1979 racing season.

In the beginning, many of the drivers had a keen distrust of Robert and some of the new and radical ideas he proposed, such as a set of uniform rules for both race cars and drivers. For example, the use of the snub nosed front ends, large rear spoilers, and a 2500 pound weight rule for car and driver. He even required racing uniforms for all the series drivers.

That first season was filled with a number of issues that had never been a part of late model dirt racing. One issue that came up at almost every track where the series promoted a race was the rule requiring drivers to wear racing suits. In many areas of the country this was something most local drivers were not accustomed to doing. Many balked at the idea because for years most drivers had worn either pants or jeans, and a T-shirt.

According to Connie Noel Melton, Robert's Secretary and Administrative Assistant, "This problem even carried over into the second season at Wythe Raceway in Wytheville, Virginia." She said, "One of the drivers got very upset when I refused to let him fill out entry

Phenix City, Alabama's Bobby Thomas, winner of the first NDRA race. Photo from the Robert Smawley Collection.

forms for the race until he had a racing suit. He later borrowed one from another driver and was then allowed to enter the race."

As mentioned, a lot of drivers on the dirt tour were skeptical of Smawley and many of his ideas. However, almost to a driver, they all wanted him to somehow succeed in making dirt track racing a sport you could make a living doing. For example, C.L. Pritchett of Cornelia, Georgia, winner of the '78 Reed Cams 100 at the Cherokee Speedway said, "After racing around on these little-bitty tracks for years, it's nice to finally get some publicity and make some decent money for winning a race." When asked how it felt to win an NDRA race, Pritchett said, "How's it feel? It feels $10,000 good."

C. L. Pritchett, winner of the '78 Reed Cams 100, felling $10,000 good. Photo from the Robert Smawley Collection.

Another Georgia driver, Charles Hughes of Dalton, Georgia, who went on to compete in several NDRA races, said about the NDRA, "Dirt racing is coming back because of Smawley's series. I know him personally and I feel he will do what he says he will." Charles went on to say, "So far he has done what he told the drivers and track owners he would do." In closing Charles said, "Drivers can now make

Charles Hughes stands beside his #39 Camaro before a race. Photo provided by Charles Hughes.

Bruce Mississippi's Jerry Inmon. Photo provided by Bobby Duke.

money running a race car, whereas before it was hard to do, if you could at all."

Finally, Jerry Inmon of Bruce, Mississippi, a fixture on the NDRA tour since its start said, "In 1978, I won more races than anybody in the country. Since then, thanks to the NDRA, I win less, but win more money." Jerry and his car owner, Dick Stevens, planned on running Smawley's tour as long as, they said, "Robert keeps doing what he says he'll do and keeps paying out the money he does on this tour." As you can see from these drivers, along with many others, they all seemed to want him and his series to be a success.

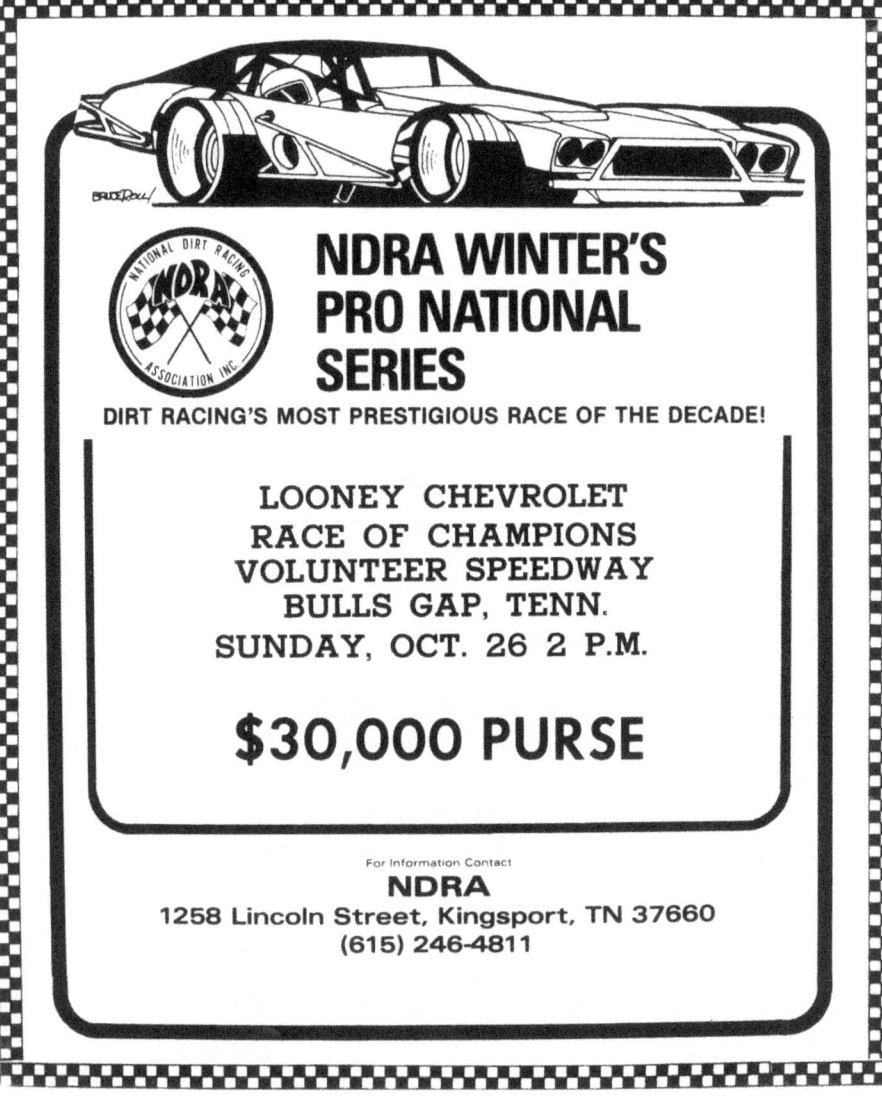

An ad for the Looney Chevrolet Race of Champions in 1978. Ad from the Robert Smawley Collection.

A lot of track owners and promoters were also skeptical of Robert. Before Smawley came along, most track owners had never turned their ticket sales and promotional duties over to anyone. This was in large part because, the ticket sales were such a large cash business. For many owners, this took a lot of getting used to. As I mentioned, there was a lot of track owner distrust toward Smawley. This was

Robert Smawley in his famous checkered flag shirt holds up the $10,000 winner's check for one of his 100 lap events. Photo from the Robert Smawley Collection.

because Robert was making big promises about the money they would be making. He also stressed the quality and large number of race cars they would be drawing, as well as the publicity they would be receiving for their racing facilities. As the old saying goes, "It all sounded too good to be true."

The "Silver Fox" David Pearson at an NDRA race with NDRA secretary Connie Noel Melton on his left. Photo provided by David Chobat.

Connie Melton told me recently, "I believe the biggest problem the track owners had with Robert was they saw a lot of themselves in him." However, as the inaugural season progressed, the distrust some track owners had for Smawley and his new dirt racing series began to lessen. This resulted from a number of owners starting to see just how successful the tracks already on the NDRA schedule were. Over the course of the season most of the problems were ironed out as the smooth talking Smawley was able to reassure them that, "All would be well." As the NDRA started to gain national acceptance by the drivers, car owners, track owners, and even the race fans, someone once asked Jerry Inmon's car owner, Dick Stevens, what he thought about the series and his answer was, "It's the best thing since sliced bread."

Early on, the national exposure of NDRA also played a big part in starting what became known as the "Racing Chassis War." This was a competition between chassis builders to see who could build the best dirt chassis and win the most races on this new national dirt series. Among the early builders were, the very popular Jig-A-Low chassis out of Phenix City, Alabama; Booneville Indiana's M.R.E.; and the Glenn Bopp Chassis out of Lonedell, Missouri. Even the "Godfather" of the asphalt chassis, Ed Howe, came South from his Beaverton, Michigan, shop to enter the world of dirt racing on the NDRA trail. This would continue throughout the rest of the series, with Whiteland Indiana's, C.J. Rayburn Race Cars; and Cowpens, South Carolina's, Barry Wright Race Cars and others joining the battle. Even today the chassis wars continue with Mooresburg, Tennessee's, Scott Bloomquist's Team Zero; and Bobby Labonte's, Longhorn Chassis, which is winning big in 2015 on the Lucas Oil Late Model Dirt Series.

Some of Robert Smawley's major sponsors that first year were: Lunati Racing Cams out of Memphis, Tennessee; Strasburg Ohio's Malcuit Racing Engines; Carrera Shocks based in Atlanta, Georgia; Hoosier Racing Tires out of Lakeville, Indiana; Barry Wright Race Cars located in Cowpens, South Carolina; and of course, Vaughn Winter

Leon Archer in Victory Lane after his first series win at Myrtle Beach, SC. Photo provided by David Chobat.

and his York Pennsylvania based Winter's Performance Products; the quick-change gear company and the first title sponsor of the racing series. Again, the NDRA gave the above racing sponsors, along with many others, a national stage to spotlight and sell their products all over the country.

Most of the drivers came on board Robert's "Greatest Show in Dirt Racing" for no other reason that the enormous purses for winning one of his 100 lap events. It seemed a lot of $5,000 and $10,000 to-win purses and other promotional incentives were there for the taking. Smawley was also a master at getting local businesses involved with his races. For example, Kingsport, Tennessee's Looney Chevrolet sponsored

Larry Moore shares a photo moment with a young race fan. Photo provided by Buddy Duke.

NASCAR star David Pearson stands beside the #81 he drove at the Pearson National Speedway race. Photo from the Robert Smawley Collection.

the $30,000 Looney Chevrolet Race of Champions, at the Volunteer Speedway in Bulls Gap, Tennessee, on October 26, 1979. That race was won by Chattanooga, Tennessee's Ronnie Johnson. Other ideas Robert put in place were having sponsors award prizes for winning the pole position. In addition, companies like Crane Cams, Weber Performance Products, and 104+ Octane became frequent players at many of Smawley's events.

Also, the NDRA pit steward "Fuzzy" C.J. Orange started what he called the "Hot Dog" award. This award was usually given to the driver who, according to "Fuzzy, " had the best performance during the race. Several drivers won this award, including Mike Duvall, and "Little" Bill Corum. "Fuzzy" said, "I even gave the award to a hobby class driver who entered an NDRA race at Wytheville one time and finished in the top 15. He won, I believe, around a $1,000 and was tickled to death."

According to Michael "Cotton" Duke, the NDRA Assistant and Robert Smawley's "right hand man," Smawley once told him, "I want to film everything: all the action at the tracks, all the activities at the motels, the pool parties, the cookouts, the pig roasts, driver introductions, driver interactions with the sponsors, the race fans, everything." What does this sound like? It sounds like "reality television" long before it was even thought of. This was a unique quality you saw in Robert.

Recently Buddy Duke said, "Robert was so far ahead of his time, he foresaw the eventual rise of cable television, and presented his idea of having his series on cable to the Nashville Network in the mid '80's. The man was simply far ahead of his time in a lot of his ideas and promotional skills."

As more and more race fans started to follow the NDRA in its first year, Smawley would bring in NASCAR stars like Harry Gant, David Pearson, and others to sign autographs for the fans. Connie Melton once told me that at the 1978 race at Myrtle Beach, South Carolina, Neil Bonnett showed up just to enjoy the race. She was in charge of ticket sales that night and did not recognize him, charging him the regular gate admission price. Later, she was at the booth where Harry

Haubstadt, Indiana's Tom Helfrich during a drivers' meeting. Photo from the Robert Smawley Collection.

Gant and the other NASCAR drivers were signing autographs for the fans. She looked around and saw Neil there also signing autographs. She said, "I felt so foolish, not recognizing him. I tried to refund his money, but he would have none of that. He laughed and said it was alright. He was a very good sport about it."

Later in an article by Dick Berggren, Smawley admitted this idea met with mixed results. Robert said he found out NASCAR fans and late model dirt fans are basically two different types of race fans. He said, although dirt fans recognized the drivers of NASCAR, it appeared to make little difference in the size of his race crowds. After this experiment, Smawley added more pageantry to his events, both before and after his races. He was quick to pick this up from the NASCAR races and the success it appeared to bring that series.

Leon Archer would go on to win his first NDRA race that night at Myrtle Beach, the "Winter's Performance 100," over Charlie Mincey, Billy Thomas, Bobby Thomas, and Jerry Inmon in that order. Evidently Leon liked that win because he went on to win the very next race at the Jackson (TN) Fairgrounds, the "Truex Chevy 100," on October 7, 1978. He beat Doug Kenimer, Bud Lunsford, Ronnie Johnson, and Roscoe Smith to the finish line in that race. This was the start of his march toward winning the NDRA's first National Championship in 1979.

However, it would not be an easy road for Archer. After a strong showing early in the tour, Leon built a new race car for the title chase. In the last race of '78, Archer qualified his new race car at Atomic (TN) Speedway's first ever NDRA race. That night his race car, along with his ramp truck, tires, and all his tools were stolen at his motel. Leon told me when I was writing the book, RED CLAY AND DUST, "That was the best handling race car I ever had." Archer said, "I had to build another race car right in the middle of the title chase. But with a lot of help from the other drivers and a lot of my friends, and a lot of blood, sweat, and tears, we were able to overcome the loss and go on and win the title."

Dayton, Ohio's Larry Moore would score the win at Atomic in his first NDRA start on October 29, 1978, in the "Racing Enterprises 100," beating Billy Thomas, Rodney Combs, Buddy Rogers, and Bud Lunsford to the checkered flag. This was one of the first NDRA races that I attended, and I was immediately hooked on Robert Smawley's new national late model dirt racing series.

Recently, Larry told me a funny story about the race at Atomic. He said, "I showed up with an ugly green race car. That along with being one of only a couple of 'Yankees' in the race was a lot to overcome down South." Moore did go on to win the race in his "ugly green" race car, and he had a good time in victory lane at one of the South's most historic dirt tracks.

After five series events, the Atomic (TN) Speedway race ended the '78 part of the 1979 season (Confusing isn't it?) As the 1979 portion of the season started, Smawley was still wondering, to himself, if the NDRA would be the success he hoped it would be. At its first '79 race on March 3, 1979, Smawley put his series to its biggest test. The Winter's Performance 100 race was scheduled at Pearson National Speedway in the tiny town of Louisville, Mississippi. The track was a small one-quarter mile race track that had seating for only about 2,000 race fans. Even worse was the track's location; it was on a dirt road, off a dirt road, off a narrow two lane paved highway, forty miles from the nearest motel, located in Starkville. Robert scheduled this race, as he said, "To see how strong I really am." To help draw race fans to the track, Smawley advertised that NASCAR star, David Pearson would be driving a car in the race. He did show up and raced but fell out before the half way mark due to mechanical problems, finishing 23rd. Through Smawley's brilliant promoting efforts, several thousand race fans showed up for the event. Most of the NDRA regulars like Buck Simmons, Rodney Combs, and Leon Archer were on hand.

Robert talking on top of a concession stand at Dixie Speedway. Photo from the Robert Smawley Collection.

In addition, you had the locals hoping the "good ole" Southern boys would prevail over the "Yankee" drivers. Northern drivers, Kenny Brightbill and Tommy Helfrich started up front, along with the crowd favorite, Jerry Inmon of Bruce, Mississippi. Inmon made a driver mistake early on and had to come from far back in the field to finish second. Jerry gave the crowd something to cheer about. They cheered loudly every time he passed a car on his charge toward the front. Ultimately, he finished second as he just ran out of laps. In the end, Washington, Georgia's, Fulmer Lance would save the day for the South, taking the $10,000 first prize. On a bitter cold night in Mississippi, the fans left happy; and Smawley had no more doubts about his series after that. He said after the Pearson race, "If I can draw a crowd like that here in the middle of nowhere and make money, then I know my series is going to be a winner."

Smawley was a genius at bringing in the race fans with his clever promotions and sales ideas. While sitting in a lawn chair on the roof of a concession stand at Dixie Speedway in Woodstock, Georgia at one of his '79 races held toward the end of the season, he waved at

Robert Smawley and Mickey Swims talk before an NDRA race. Photo from the Robert Smawley Collection.

fans coming to find a seat two hours early. The fans waved and hollered back at Robert, wishing him well. He turned to one of the track officials sitting with him and said, "When the fans start wishing the promoter well, he pretty much knows he has everyone on his side."

In another of Smawley's innovative ideas, his NDRA tour was one of the first to make use of the souvenir trailer to sell drivers T-shirts, hats, and other racing souvenir items to the race fans. I recently talked with Fred Vineyard and his sister Betty Vineyard-Price. This brother and sister team, along with Betty's husband, Darwin "Shon" Price, were the ones who started selling the official NDRA souvenirs for Smawley at all the series races. (Several photos that pertain to the souvenir trailer and the beginning of the racing souvenirs can be found in the back of the book photos starting on page 159.)

Betty said, "We started out selling NDRA items out of a van. However, it didn't take us long before we realized we needed a trailer because of the big demand for NDRA souvenirs." She continued, "What better job could anyone have, traveling the country with your husband and kids and meeting a lot of great people."

The Rock-em, Sock-em, Travelin' Sideways Dirt Show

As the NDRA grew during the first few years, from 13 races the first year, to 28 races for the '81 season, Smawley was making national late model stars out of regional drivers. The drivers were enjoying the limelight as more and more drivers decided to join the National Dirt Racing Association and its "Traveling Dirt Show."

The series also changed the dirt late model race fans. They were now thinking of late model dirt racing on the national level, instead of just locally or regionally as had been the case since its beginnings in the late 1950's.

As the track owners saw the rapid growth of the series and the money being made by both the series drivers and the tracks, owners from all over the country were now eager to sign on to Smawley's, "Rock-em, Sock-em, Travelin' Sideways Dirt Show."

One of the first promoters to sign on with Smawley in Georgia was the legendary Southern promoter, Mickey Swims. Swims owned two dirt tracks in the metro Atlanta area: Dixie Speedway, located in Woodstock, Georgia; and the big half mile Rome Speedway in nearby Rome, Georgia. I have known Mickey for years, and he has always had the uncanny ability to foresee an opportunity in racing and take it. He scheduled NDRA races for both his tracks, and they became very successful stops on the tour. Mickey recently told me, "I always liked Robert Smawley and his ideas and promotions. Sometimes, though, I'd have to tone him down a bit with his activities during his NDRA events." Swims continued with a laugh, "I'd tell him to, 'Keep it family rated, Robert'."

The NDRA had its share of what was known as the "regular" series drivers like Simmons, Archer, Moore, Combs, and Inmon. However, that first season saw a number of local drivers score wins on the tour. Among them were: C.L. Pritchett at Gaffney, South Carolina's, Cherokee Speedway; H.E. Vineyard at Bull's Gap, Tennessee's, Volunteer Speedway; and Tommy Joe Pauschert at Van Buren, Arkansas' Crawford County Speedway. Ironically, this turned out to be all those drivers' first and only wins on the NDRA tour.

Leon Archer scored the most first season wins with three. That included the last race of the inaugural season held at Anderson (SC)

Leon Archer talks with Robert Smawley after Leon clinched the NDRA title at Anderson (SC) Speedway. Photo provided by David Chobat.

Motor Speedway, won by Leon over Larry Moore, Rodney Combs, and Bud Lunsford, on his way to the 1979 NDRA Points Championship. Buck Simmons and Rodney Combs had two victory lane appearances each.

Perhaps Smawley's biggest accomplishment that first year was, as he put it, "I professionalized dirt track racing for the first time in its history." In doing so he also made professionals out of his touring dirt late model drivers. In turn they benefited from the NDRA, most making more money than they had ever made previously in dirt racing. For example, not including the last '79 race at Dixie Speedway, Rodney Combs earned $77,000; Larry Moore won $76,000; and Leon Archer had put almost $70,000 in his bank account. The '79 NDRA season had a total purse of $420,000, not bad for a first year late model dirt circuit. It was just an unheard of amount to earn at that time.

The Rock-em, Sock-em, Travelin' Sideways Dirt Show

Smawley is all smiles after receiving the Promoter of the Year Award from the NDRA drivers. Leon Archer and Buck Simmons presented the award. Photo from the Robert Smawley Collection.

At the end of that first year, Smawley was presented with The Promoter of the Year Award by the drivers of the series. The award was presented by the 1979 NDRA points champion, Leon Archer and one of the series' star drivers, Buck Simmons.

The beginnings of national exposure was evident, as the series promoted races in several states that first year. Those states were: Georgia, Alabama, Tennessee, Mississippi, South Carolina, North Carolina, and Arkansas.

1979 Final NDRA Points Standing

1. Leon Archer, Griffin, GA (3998)
2. Buck Simmons, Baldwin, GA (3618)
3. Bobby Thomas, Phenix City, ALA (3244)
4. Billy Thomas, Phenix City, ALA (3148)
5. Doug Kenimer, Dahlonega, GA (3062)

The NDRA Series Points Champions

Chapter Four

The NDRA Series Points Champions

This chapter takes a look at all six of the NDRA's points champions, with a focus on the NDRA portion of their dirt racing careers, along with the path each driver took on the road to the series points title. Also, as we discuss each of these NDRA Champions, you, the reader, will learn a lot about the history of Smawley's national dirt touring series, as we take a year by year look at each of these outstanding dirt late model drivers.

Leon Archer
NDRA Series Points Champion 1979

From a weekend dirt warrior, to becoming the National Dirt Racing Association's (NDRA) first National Champion, that's what Griffin, Georgia's Leon Archer was able to accomplish in 1979. The road to the title was not as easy as his win in the "Winter's 100 at Anderson (SC) Speedway, the last race of the 13 race NDRA schedule for '79. All he had to do was complete the first lap of the race and the title would be his. He not only made that first lap, but went on to take the victory in a race loaded with NDRA stars. However, the championship was almost lost when Archer's ramp truck, along with his #222 race car, were stolen at an NDRA race at Atomic Speedway in Knoxville, Tennessee in October of '78. Leon said he had to build a complete new race car right in the middle of the points chase. Archer said, "Without the help of many in the racing community, I could not have built a race car and won the championship, and for that I am very thankful to all the people that helped me."

That first NDRA Championship had an odd beginning and ending schedule. The season didn't start until August 5, 1978, with a race at Phenix City, Alabama's East Alabama Motor Speedway, won by Bobby Thomas. The series ended on June 30, 1979, in the race at the Anderson (SC) Motor Speedway, mentioned above. Smawley knew

Leon Archer in his #222 after one of his many victories. Photo provided by Leon Archer.

he had to get his schedule in line with the regular racing season. He did so the next season by taking the remainder of '79 and all of the 1980 season and awarded a 1980 series champion at the end of that season. The last race of the '80 NDRA season was held at Volunteer Speedway at Bull's Gap, Tennessee, won by Freddy Smith. After that the championships were awarded at the end of the regular season.

Leon Archer was one of those drivers who always liked strong competition. During his early career he would travel to tracks where the competition was the toughest. On one occasion he told me, "I knew I could win close to home at tracks like West Atlanta Raceway or the Senoia Speedway. So I started going to a little track in Cummings, Georgia, known as 'The Mountain.' The races there were hard to win because drivers like Leon Sells, Buck Simmons, and Jody Ridley were usually there. Heck, Buck Simmons usually had a 'bounty' on him." After hearing of Smawley's NDRA series, with its $10,000 to win races, Archer was like so many other local drivers who were eager to test their skills against drivers from other parts of the country.

The Rock-em, Sock-em, Travelin' Sideways Dirt Show

Leon Archer -
From 'Sunday Driving' To A National Championship
By Greg Fielden

SURFSIDE BEACH, S.C. - Leon Archer (Griffin, Ga.) is the first NDRA (National Dirt Racing Association) national champion and stands to collect $10,000 for winning the title.

The 39-year-old Archer was triumphant in three NDRA championship events including the "Winter's 100" at Anderson, S.C., the finale of the first 13-race schedule which began last summer.

Archer is one of the finest representatives of Southern dirt track stock car racing and he will wear the crown well.

"I am very proud to be the first NDRA champion," Archer said graciously. "And I am thankful to Robert Hawley for doing what he has done for dirt track racing."

Archer assumed command in the lucrative points race after the third event on the schedule, which was held at Myrtle Beach Speedway last Labor Day weekend.

"We really had the car running good and we were able to win the race after we got the right tires on the car," said Archer. "We had run pretty good in the first two races, but we really got things going at Myrtle Beach."

He bagged his second straight win in the "Truex Chevy 100" at Jackson, Tenn.

A couple of weeks later, his powerful #222 Camaro, tow truck and many spare parts aboard were stolen from a motel parking lot the night before the "Roscoe's

Archer wins the last race of '79 NDRA season to clinch the series first points championship. Article provided by Greg Fielden. Photo by David Chobat.

SOUTHERN AUTO RACING NEWS
Vol. IX No. 3   75¢   July 30, 1981

Archer Returns To NDRA Limelight

BY PAUL MCLAIN
Morristown, TN

BULLS GAP, TN (July 25) - Leon Archer found a rough road ahead after being crowned the first NDRA champion, but after a two-year lapse between national victories in the NDRA circuit, tonight at Volunteer Speedway the Schlitz Pro National Looney Chevrolet 100 belonged to the Griffin, GA, veteran. Archer, who capped the first NDRA season with a win in the June race at Anderson, SC, found tonight's victory especial- pulled even with Simmons going into turn four took the lead going down the frontstraight. The former champion pulled away to settle the issue of the winner, making sure the victory was his.

From there on, the battle from second to fifth was a real war as the rest of the field swapped positions every few laps.

In victory lane ceremonies, Archer said, "I ran out of brakes early but they came back. The traffic was rough tonight; I didn't know which way to go.

"But when Buck and while Fulmer Lance brought Rick Mattson's p00ls Camaro home fifth.

Jack Boggs, Don Hester, Tootle Estes in Darrell Monk's #45, Pete Parker and Jerry Inmon completed the top 10.

Mike Duvall, who won the NDRA championship race in Hagerstown, MD, was running fourth when a broken oil pump put him out on lap 59.

L.D. Ottinger blew an engine in Friday night's heat races but came back to win the 50-lap consolation and advance to the feature, where he finished 11th. Randy Boggs was se-

Leon Archer returned to his winning ways in the NDRA after a two-year dry spell by besting the field at Bulls Gap, TN. (Wayne Kindness photo)

Leon scores his last NDRA career win at the Volunteer Speedway in July of '81. Courtesy of *Southern Auto News*. Story by Paul McClain. photo by Wayne Kindness.

Leon started the inaugural NDRA season in '78 by winning his first series race on September 2nd at Myrtle Beach (SC) Speedway, the Winter's Performance 100. Archer told me, "Most races I ran at the tracks around Atlanta were 30 or 40 laps, sometimes a 50 lapper. I had never thought of wearing a set of tires out in a race. So we had no extra tires at Myrtle Beach." He went on to say, "By the time they threw the caution at lap 50 of the 100 lap race, my tires were finished. The car had a set of Firestone 125's on it. This was the tire most of the local drivers were racing on at the tracks back home. The local Goodyear rep saw my situation, and he gave me a set of asphalt slicks." Leon then said, "I believe I was running third at the time, but when I put those Goodyear tires on, and the green came back out, it was like I was a train on rails. I went to the front and won the race, and $10,000, the most I had ever won for a race."

Leon then won the very next race, the Truex Chevy 100, at the Jackson (TN) Fairgrounds on October 7th. He went on to win the '79 series points title over Baldwin, Georgia's Buck Simmons, and Phenix City, Alabama drivers, Bobby and Billy Thomas.

After the Anderson win, where he clinched his points championship, he had a long dry spell on the NDRA tour. In May of '81, Barry Wright and Archer teamed up, with Leon driving the Barry Wright/ Carolina Tool and Equipment Company race car. It took only two months before he was back in victory lane, winning the Schlitz Pro National Looney Chevrolet 100 at Bull's Gap, Tennessee's Volunteer Speedway on July 25, 1981. This was Archer's fourth and final NDRA win of his career.

Archer enjoyed the spotlight the series brought to the drivers, making them national stars on the dirt racing scene. He also liked the big racing purses Smawley paid for his NDRA races. Leon Archer proved he was one of those Georgia drivers, like Buck Simmons, Stan Massey, and Bud Lunsford, who could run with the nation's best dirt late model drivers of the time.

Leon was one of the few dirt late model drivers to race his entire career in that tough division. During his career he would win over 250 feature races. Archer received the ultimate honor a dirt late model driver can achieve, when he was inducted into the National Dirt Late

Model Hall of Fame in 2003. However, Leon Archer will always be remembered as the hard charging driver of the triple digit #222 from Griffin, Georgia.

Larry Moore
NDRA Series Points Champion 1980

Dayton, Ohio's Larry Moore knows race cars inside and out; he is the "racer's racer." Moore recently told me, "I've run almost every type of race car imaginable. They've been mainly stock cars, in run-what-you-brung races. But I've also drove sprints and sprint modifieds." He went on to say, "I was associated with USAC from 1972 until 1978. I won three USAC events during that time." Larry said in closing, "My biggest win, as I call it, came at the Trenton, New Jersey race, when I beat A.J. Foyt to the checkered flag."

According to some who know him, he has the uncanny ability to seemingly become part of the race car he is driving. His body feels everything the car's chassis does. It's like his brain is hooked to the

Larry Moore celebrates with Robert Smawley and the trophy queens after an NDRA win. Photo provided by David Chobat.

Some of the race cars Moore drove during the NDRA series. Photo from an NDRA yearbook.

engine and the tires he has chosen for the race. Moore feels like he is part of the car. This ability is what carried Larry to the 1980 NDRA Points Championship, the longest, time wise, in the series history. Actually, the '80 season started on July 14, 1979, at the Wytheville Raceway in Wytheville, Virginia and ran until the end of the '80 season

Moore's Tri-City Aluminum red #14 in action. Photo provided by dirtfans.com.

on October 26th at the Volunteer Speedway in Bull's Gap, Tennessee. After the '79 and '80 NDRA seasons, Smawley adjusted the schedule to run during the regular racing season, starting in the Spring and ending in the Fall.

On October 29, 1978, Moore burst upon the NDRA racing scene at Atomic Speedway, located near Knoxville, Tennessee. Larry told me recently, "I had two things going against me that day. I think I was the only 'Yankee' in the lineup that day, and I was driving an ugly green race car." He went on to say, "After I won my first NDRA race at Atomic that day, I didn't know how the good ole Southern boys were going to accept a Yankee winning in a green race car." He managed to leave the Southern track alive that day and was a terror on the NDRA circuit for the rest of it's colorful run into dirt racing's history.

The 1979 season saw Larry, in the legendary Ed Howe chassis, Bobby Paul pipe line #P1 race car, score more than 25 wins and set at least 16 track records on race tracks they had never competed on. In addition, Moore went on to score the first of his three World 100 wins; the others being, '81 and again in '85.

During Moore's 1980 NDRA championship season, he started the year in Bobby Paul's #P1 race car, but only a short time into the season, Bobby Paul Racing split with Moore. Larry then became a car owner for the first time, aligning himself with legendary car builder, C.J. Rayburn. He then unveiled his signature golden-yellow #1M Rayburn race car for the remainder of the '80 season.

Moore started the '79 portion of the 1980 season by winning, two of the first five NDRA races. He won the 100 lap Cam 2 event at Pearson National Speedway in Louisville, Mississippi on August 4th. His next win came two weeks later at his home state track, Portsmouth, Ohio's Southern Ohio Raceway, in the Stock Car Fiberglass 100 on August 18, 1979.

Ironically, Stock Car Fiberglass would become one of his sponsors on the new Rayburn car after he and Bobby Paul severed ties early in the 1980 racing season. Since that breakup, Moore worked hard to break in the new #1M car and maintain his NDRA points lead. The winners circle was hard to find during the rest of the '80 season. It was August 9th before Larry again found victory lane on the tour, winning the middle night of the NDRA's Super Dirt Weekend. He won the NDRA Lunati Cams 100 at the Magnolia Speedway (Spencer) in Tupelo, Mississippi.

Again consistency proved the winning formula, as Moore scored only three wins on the 24 race tour in 1980. However, 10 second place finishes, 3 third place finishes, and a fourth, along with only four finishes out of the top ten, proved to be good enough to secure the NDRA's second series points title for Larry Moore.

In 1981 Moore teamed up with Tri-City Aluminum owner, Jim Erp, to form a racing team and hired Georgia late model star, Buck Simmons, to drive a second team car. Moore and Erp then took advantage of Larry Moore's skills on chassis design and started the Erp and Moore Racing Company, located in Ocala, Florida. Moore then built an innovative race car, with the team colors changing from golden-yellow to a bright red. Moore's new number was his old sprint car #14, while Buck was also driving a red car with his familiar #41 on its side.

With his new car and team, Moore had almost instant success in '81. He started the season off by winning the Daytona Winter Nationals, along with six NDRA wins, the '81 World 100 (becoming the first repeat winner), and scored a $15,000 victory the following week in the Southern 100 at the Southern Ohio Raceway.

Moore, along with fellow teammate Simmons, made 1981 perhaps the most successful year by a racing team that the NDRA would see during its almost eight year run. Together they had a total of 17 checkered flags between them; Moore had six, while Simmons had an amazing eleven wins as he marched toward the '81 NDRA points title.

After the '81 season, Larry would go on to score six more NDRA wins in '82, and the final two victories of his NDRA career came in 1983. His last NDRA victory lane appearance was on July 30, in the Childs & Albert National 100 at Wythe Raceway in Wytheville, Virginia. Also, in '83 he had his highest series points finish after his points title in '80, finishing third. According to *Dirt on Dirt*, Moore would go on to finish second on the NDRA all time wins list with 18 victories.

Some of Larry Moore's other wins and accomplishments after the NDRA include: the '84 Hillbilly 100; a third World 100 in '85; the '87 Dirt Track World Championship; and the '87 STARS National Series Championship. Moore raced dirt late models into the mid-90's. According to Larry, he last raced competitively in 2004. During his career in racing, Moore had over 500 wins to his credit. He was inducted into the National Dirt Late Model Hall of Fame in its first year of 2001.

Today, Larry Moore lives in Florida. He has recently released a book entitled, ON TOP OF THE WORLD. The book tells the story of Larry's career in racing. The book has a very good section about his time in the NDRA.

Larry Moore is a fun guy to be around and talk racing with. In closing, I'll borrow one of his most famous phrases to best describe him, "He was one helluva race driver."

Buck Simmon
NDRA Series Points Champion 1981

I saw Baldwin, Georgia's Buck Simmons for the first time at Dixie Speedway in Woodstock, Georgia at the start of the 1970 season. I was a member of Jody Ridley's pit crew at the time, and we came to Dixie to see where we stacked up against this regional late model dirt star. Simmons had been winning races all over the region and

Buck Simmons standing beside the #41 before an NDRA race. Photo provided by Al Eaves.

The Rock-em, Sock-em, Travelin' Sideways Dirt Show

Buck celebrates with Smawley and trophy queen, Eva Taylor, after a win in the Darrel Monk #41. Photo provided by Michael Edwards.

especially in the metro Atlanta area. For example, during Dixie Speedway's inaugural season in 1969, he won an amazing 18 of the first 22 races at the track in his legendary Speedy Evans/Da-Je Homes #41 Chevelle. So it came as no surprise that he would have a successful racing career in Robert Smawley's NDRA series.

Buck ran all the NDRA series races in '79, winning his first series race at Phenix City, Alabama's East Alabama Motor Speedway on March 31st of that year. He finished second in the first year's points battle to the eventual winner and fellow Georgian, Leon Archer. Most of Simmons' early series races were in Darrel Monk's Carrie Coal Company #41 race car. While driving for Monk, Buck once said of Smawley's new national dirt series, "I want to run all the races Robert Smawley promotes." Simmons continued, "And I think anyone with a competitive car should support Smawley. If not for Smawley, we'd still be running for peanuts. He has helped racing all over the country."

However, for many years Simmons had dreamed of a career in NASCAR and the feel of running at 190 mph. In 1979 that dream came true, as Kenny Childers gave him a NASCAR Cup Series ride. Buck ran eight Cup Series races; his best finish was a 14th at Atlanta Motor Speedway in '79. After a short stint in the Childers car, Buck left NASCAR and returned to his first love, dirt racing. Simmons cited several reasons for leaving the Cup Series. Chief among them were, according to Buck, "I couldn't afford to go off and stay all week. I didn't have the experience to tell them what to do with the car, and some of the crew were not experienced enough to know what to do without the driver's input."

Buck's lack of experience in setting up a race car was colorfully described by former NDRA pit steward, "Fuzzy" Orange in a recent phone conversation I had with him. "Fuzzy" said, "Buck's idea of race car set up was, climb in, set down, wiggle your ass in the seat til you were comfortable, strap yourself in; and then he would lean forward and tell the car that it was going to be his [Buck's] best friend tonight." This inability to set a race car up was later brought up by a fellow driver and former Jim Erp teammate, Larry Moore. Moore said, "I didn't realize how little Buck knew about race car set-ups until I was around him. No matter what was done to the car, Buck always drove it the same. Most drivers set the car for their driving style. Buck adapted his driving style to whatever the car was doing. No matter – he was a helluva driver."

Buck continued to drive for Darrel Monk during the '79 and the early part of the '80 season on the NDRA tour. Keep in mind, what was called the 1980 NDRA season had an odd starting and finishing date. The season ran from mid-July '79 through the entire 1980 racing season. Buck Simmons wasted no time, winning the '80 season's opening series race at the Wythe Raceway in Wytheville, Virginia on July 14, 1979.

It was during the 1980 season that Simmons would become the teammate of Rodney Combs on Jim Erp's Tri-City Aluminum race team out of Ocala, Florida. On paper, it appeared to be the dream team of the NDRA. They even had identical race cars, Buck drove the red #41, while Rodney drove the red #5. Later, in the '80 season the Tri-City Aluminum duo each won back to back NDRA races. Combs scored his wins at Granite City, Illinois' Tri-City Speedway on June 21st

The Rock-em, Sock-em, Travelin' Sideways Dirt Show

and at Volusia Speedway Park in Barberville, Florida on July 3rd. Buck Simmons saw his two checkered flags at Bulls Gap, Tennessee's Volunteer Speedway on July 26th, and at the Jackson (TN) Fairgrounds on August 8th. Simmons would go on to score his final 1980 victory lane appearance at one of his favorite tracks, the Dixie Speedway on October 5th. Buck finished fourth in the series point battle in 1980, behind NDRA Series Points Champion, Dayton, Ohio's Larry Moore.

In 1981 there was no stopping Simmons as he marched toward the series points title, which was now known as the "NDRA/Schlitz Pro-National Series." On his way to the championship, Buck had only three bad finishes. He finished 19th twice and 21st once. In the races he didn't win, he finished second four times, third four times, fourth three times, and had one 14th. Of the 28 NDRA races, he finished in the top four 24 times, a feat that was never matched by any other series driver.

In the second race of the season on April 25th, at Maryville, Tennessee's Smoky Mountain Raceway, now driving for the Erp and Moore race team, Simmons scored the first of his eleven wins that season (according to *Dirt on Dirt*). For the most part, Buck dominated the '81 season, winning four races in a row at one point. Those four victories were: August 14, Log Cabin Raceway and Park, in Rocky Mount, VA; August 16, Wythe Raceway, at Wytheville, VA; August 20, the Sante Fe Speedway, in Willow Springs, ILL; and finally, Paducah (KY) International Raceway on August 22nd. Other wins that year were at: North Alabama Speedway on May 22nd; another win at Paducah, Kentucky on June 13th; Union, Kentucky's Florence Speedway on June 19th; a holiday event (my wife and I attended this race) at Atomic (TN) Speedway on July 3rd; and Georgetown, Delaware's Seacoast Speedway on July 15. He won his last race of his '81 championship season at a track closer to his Baldwin, Georgia hometown, the Anderson (SC) Motor Speedway on September 7, 1981.

After his '81 championship season, Buck would go on to score wins in three more NDRA events. In 1982 he had back-to-back wins at Portsmouth, Ohio's Southern Ohio Raceway (where Kentucky's "Black" Jack Boggs started his early late model career) on August 6th; and at K-C Raceway at Chillicothe, Ohio the very next day on August

7th. His best points finish after the '81 season was a fourth in Mike Duvall's NDRA Championship season of 1982.

His last NDRA series win, on October 13, 1985, proved to be one of the biggest wins of his career. In what Buck described as, "A Helluva day." He not only won the $20,000 winner's share of the 2nd Annual $250,000 NDRA/Stroh's Invitational at the Kingsport Speedway; Simmons also claimed the $10,000 Dutch Treats Pole Award for fast qualifier. Buck, representing I-85 Raceway in Greer, South Carolina, drove his Barry Wright/Carolina Tools late model to the win over Tommy Joe Pauschert, collecting a $30,000 total winner's share in one of Smawley's biggest NDRA events. Simmons is the all-time NDRA wins leader with 20 Checkered flags, according to *Dirt on Dirt*. However, some sources list his win total at 23.

After his NDRA days, Simmons would go on to win hundreds of races all over the country. He drove for Carnesville, Georgia's Gerald Voyles for the last few years of his career, in the John Deere green #41. He had his 1000th victory celebration at the Lavonia (GA) Speedway in May of 2002. He won the last 31 races of his 1,012 career victories for Voyles. On August 12, 2012, the late model dirt racing world lost one of its all-time greats, when the legendary Charles Leroy "Buck" Simmons passed away. In my opinion, Buck was the best late model dirt driver ever to strap himself into a race car. He was just born with the natural talent to drive a race car.

Mike Duvall
NDRA Series Points Champion 1982

It began at the Lavonia (GA) Speedway during a Schlitz/NDRA points race on May 3, 1981. Dick Murphy's yellow #54 race car, with a picture of Fred Flintstone on the hood, was driven to victory by a South Carolina late model driver by the name of Mike Duvall. He had been a well known dirt late model star for years throughout the Georgia and South Carolina region. However, it took both Murphy and Duvall to make this race team click. This was the beginning of the famous Flintstone Flyer race car. At the time, the car had the distinction of being one of the first race cars to use a letter for a number, thus the

Simmons accepts the $10,000 fast qualifier award from Dutch Treats at the '85 NDRA/Stroh's Invitational at the Kingsport Speedway. Photo from Nelson Redd article.

#F1 in flyer. In 1982, the Palmetto state's Mike Duvall would go on to become the NDRA's fourth different series points champion, driving the now famous yellow and red Flintstone Flyer.

1982 was one of the best years for Robert Smawley's NDRA traveling dirt series. The year saw Kentucky's Jack Boggs score a win for the NDRA drivers in the "Super Bowl of Dirt Racing," held inside the Pontiac Silverdome. It also saw a 20 year old rookie by the name of Donnie Moran win the richest dirt race in history (up to that time) on September 24th, taking home an unheard of $35,000 at the Log Cabin Raceway and Park in Rocky Mount, Virginia. The year even had a UFO winning an NDRA race, as driver Wayne Brooks in the #UFO took the checkered flag over Jeff Purvis, Buck Simmons and Jack Boggs at I-30 Speedway in Little Rock, Arkansas on June 30th.

However, Mike Duvall was a determined racer in '82. His determination paid off, as he won the NDRA/Schlitz title, driving the Flex-

A-Foam sponsored Flintstone Flyer. The bearded driver from South Carolina, with his trademark big black hat, ran 24 of the 25 races on his way to the Crown. He missed only one race and that was due to a mechanical problem. Of the 24 starts, Duvall won three, finished second four times, third twice, had seven fourth place finishes and one fifth place. He finished in the top five in 17 of the 24 NDRA races he competed in.

Those consistent high finishes gave Mike a 502 point winning margin over Rodney Combs in one of the most exciting points battles of the NDRA series. The two late model warriors dueled back and forth the whole '82 season, before Duvall was able to take the points lead late in the season and hold off the West Virginia driver for the Title. Although, Combs was the leading money and wins leader for the year, it was Duvall's consistency that won the $20,000 national championship for him.

Some of the highlights of Mike's Championship season included taking until July 24th to score his first '82 win at a 100 lap race at Puducah (KY) Raceway, besting Buck Simmons at the finish line in

Mike Duvall, the '82 NDRA Points Champion in the Flintstone Flyer race car. Photo from the Robert Smawley collection.

Duvall at an NDRA drivers' meeting in his trademark black hat. Photo from the Robert Smawley collection.

an exciting race. August 22nd, Duvall passing Simmon's #41 with only 13 laps to go in winning the Schoenfeld 100 at Thunderbird Speedway, located in Muskogee, Oklahoma. Finally, Mike was able to regain and hold the points lead, by winning the Carrie Coal 100 at Atomic Speedway in Knoxville, Tennessee on September 18th, once again finishing ahead of Buck Simmons. It has happened many times in racing, "Consistency does pay off."

The Flintstone Flyer would go onto become one of the fan favorites and a star on the NDRA tour, finishing fourth (according to *Dirt on Dirt*) on the all time wins list with 14 checkered flags to his credit. He also was the winner of one of Smawley's biggest series promotions, the Lunati Cams $50,000 bonus. This was paid out to a driver who could win three hard earned NDRA events in a row. It didn't take the South Carolina driver long before he took this big money prize home to Gaffney.

During the remainder of the NDRA series, Duvall would go on to win two more races in '83 at Nazareth (PA) Speedway on June 5th. He won the final race of the season at Concord (NC) Motorsports Park, a track he would enjoy a lot of success on during his later career. In 1984 Mike would tie Clarksville, Tennessee's Jeff Purvis for the most wins that year, with five victory lane appearances each. Duvall's wins were back-to- back wins at Perry County Speedway in Hazard, Kentucky on June 9th, and at Tri-County Speedway in Haubstadt, Indiana on June 23th. Later, he won three in a row at 81 Speedway in Odessa, Missouri on July 21st; the Kingsport (TN) Speedway on August 9th; and his final NDRA win came at the Hartsville-Darlington (SC) Speedway on

August 31st. Mike would go on to finish second in the points in '84 to Jeff Purvis. He finished fourth in points in '83 to Rodney Combs, in his only other top five points finish after his '82 Championship.

Duvall would continue his winning ways after the NDRA series ended in 1985. He won an amazing 1026 races during his career. He would end up winning the super late model points championship at Cherokee Speedway in Gaffney, South Carolina, his home track, in his final season of racing in 2008. Mike was inducted into the National Dirt Late Model Hall of Fame in 2001, in the Hall's inaugural class.

Today, Duvall teaches dirt late model racing at his Mike Duvall Racing School in Cowpens, South Carolina, which opened in 1993. It is one of the most popular driving schools in the country, graduating hundreds of drivers over the years. One thing that I have noticed recently when talking to Mike; he takes great pride in teaching his sons, Jonathan and Mitchell, his secrets to dirt racing. Don't be surprised if another "Flintstone Flyer" appears on the racing scene soon, maybe even two.

Rodney Combs
NDRA Series Points Champion 1983

Cincinnati, Ohio, born Rodney Combs is another of those late model drivers, like Georgia's Jody Ridley, who was able to adapt his driving skills to both the asphalt and dirt tracks of the country, having a successful career on both.

We will briefly mention Rodney's NASCAR career, since our main focus for this book is dirt and the NDRA. He had 55 NASCAR Sprint Cup starts over an eight year period. His first and last starts were in the Atlanta Journal 500 (1982/1990) at Atlanta International Raceway. His NASCAR Xfinity Series career consisted of 116 races over a nine year period. Rodney had 14 top tens. His best finish was an 11th in 1995. His first Xfinity race was the '82 Miller Time 300 at Charlotte Motor Speedway, and his last series race was the '97 BellSouth Mobility/Opryland 320 at Nashville. Finally, Combs had a 2 year stint in the NASCAR Camping World Truck Series, competing in 8 races. Rodney

Rodney Combs stands beside his J.D. Stacy #5 during driver introductions at an NDRA race. Photo from the Robert Smawley collection.

had 2 top tens in that series. His first race was the '95 Sears Auto Center 125 at Milwaukee, and his last series race was in '96 at the Lowe's 250 at the old North Wilkesboro Speedway

Combs started driving late models in 1968, running about a half dozen races. In the beginning, he would run well during the heat races, but in the features he would usually fail to finish due to a mechanical problems. After a brief year in Hobby Stocks in 1969, where he won a Sports Sedan Series Championship, he returned to the late model ranks in 1970. In 1971-72, Rodney ran dirt with some success; one of his biggest wins was the Tri-County 100 Season Championship at Cincinnati, Ohio.

In 1974, he switched to asphalt racing with car owner Bobby Paul. Rodney said, "Paul had a dirt car also, and we kept hearing about Smawley's big NDRA 'test' race at the Newport (TN) Speedway, so we went down to run in that race."

Recently, I talked to the NDRA scorekeeper, Chris Bowles. He told me, "That first race was actually a test race to see how one of Robert's

NDRA events would go." He also had a second "test" race in July of '78. These races were held before the first official NDRA race at Phenix City, Alabama's, East Alabama Motor Speedway on August 5th of '78. Combs said, "After the Newport races we decided to compete on dirt full time because of the money."

Rodney's first two NDRA wins came in the 1979 season, winning the Holly Automotive 100 on May 5th at the Golden Isles Speedway in Brunswick, Georgia. His second victory lane appearance was in the Reed Cam 100 at Concord, North Carolina's Motorsports Park on May 26th. Later, Combs starting driving for Dick White, who owns M.L.M Corporation and West Virginia Solar Company, both located in Weston, West Virginia. Rodney, along with his mechanic, Mark Richards, moved to a 35-acre farm in Lost Creek, West Virginia to join forces with White in forming (White/Richards/Combs) W.R.C. Racing Enterprises. Rodney would race the Howe cars, specifying that every car he raced would be for sale.

The long 1980 NDRA season (mid-1979 through all of '80 season) saw Combs score the first of his five season victories at the Summerville (SC) Speedway's Carrera Shocks 100 on September 1, 1979. Other wins in '80 included: the Southern Fall Nationals at Jackson (TN) Fairgrounds on October 20, 1979; Granite City Illinois' Bopp Chassis 100 at Tri-City Speedway on June 21, 1980; this was followed by a July 3rd win at Barberville Florida's Volusia Speedway Park's Hoosier 100 over two Florida drivers, runner-up Wayne Shugart, followed by Tommy Riggins in third. Rodney's last victory lane appearance in the '80 NDRA season was in Yankee land on October 10th at the MRE Eastern Classic 100, held at Rolling Wheels Raceway Park in Elbridge, New York.

Larry Moore would score only three NDRA wins during the '80 Season. However, Moore proved consistency does pay off, winning the 1980 points title.

Buck Simmons dominated the 1981 NDRA season, claiming the points title along with eleven victory lane appearances. This became perhaps the most successful season of any on the NDRA's championship trail.

Rodney Combs drove this Tri-City Camaro to victory in the MRE Eastern Classic 100 NDRA race at Rolling Wheels Raceway in New York. (Greg Fielden photo)

Combs Wins MRE Eastern Classic

Combs wins MRE Eastern Classic. Photo provided by Bob Markos.

The '81 season again saw Rodney Combs concentrate on Winter racing in Australia, as he had done since 1978. Rodney had a very successful racing career in Australia. He recently told me that during that career, which began in 1978 and lasted until 1993, he won over a 1000 "match races." Combs said, "I was perhaps the most recognizable American race driver during this time, even more than Richard Petty." The 1981 season on the NDRA tour proved to somewhat an uneventful one for Combs. However, he did score a number of big wins. Among them were a Southeastern Winter Nationals win at Volusia (FLA) Speedway, and a 100 lap victory at the Newport (TN) Speedway.

1982 proved to be one of Rodney's best NDRA seasons. Combs, in the J.D. Stacy red and white Firebird, was the series wins leader with seven victories, including five of the first seven races. One of his biggest wins of the '82 season occurred at the Smoky Mountain Speedway in Maryville, Tennessee, in the World's Fair 100. There he beat Leon Archer, Buck Simmons, Jack Boggs, and Mike Duvall to the finish line in that order, winning a $6,000 payday. The last of his seven wins came on August 25th at I-30 Speedway in Little Rock, Arkansas.

Rodney Combs' J.D. Stacy #5 Firebird. Photo provided by Rodney Combs.

He was also the leading money winner, pocketing $46,650 for the season. All in all, Combs was perhaps the hottest driver on the tour during '82. Rodney finished in the top five 16 times, and he had an amazing 19 top ten finishes in the 24 race schedule that year. A championship season, right? Wrong.

Despite all this success, Combs lost the points title to Mike Duvall by 502 points. Rodney said, "I missed the last two NDRA events that year and that probably cost me the title." This was the second time he had finished in the runner-up spot. The other time being his second place finish to Larry Moore in 1980. I talked to Combs recently and he said, "I was racing quite a bit in Australia during the NDRA and it probably cost me a couple of points titles." He went on to say, "I was racing three or four times a week and winning quite a lot down there. At the time, winter racing in Australia was where my focus was."

Rodney's continued success on the NDRA tour finally paid off in 1983. He was crowned the '83 NDRA/Stroh's Super Series Points Champion. It was the beer company's first year as the series' major sponsor. Consistency and running all 14 events was the key to Combs winning the points title. He drove his J.W. Hunt, Howe racing #5 to his only '83 win on June 18th at Southern Ohio Raceway. The Portsmouth, Ohio event earned Rodney a $5,000 payday out of the $30,000

Rodney Combs leading the pack during an NDRA race. Photo from the Robert Smawley collection.

event. Ironically, this was his last NDRA win. According to *Dirt on Dirt*, Combs finished third on the all time NDRA wins list with 15 victory lane appearances.

Combs would go on to win a number of high profile races during the remainder of his dirt career, racing dirt into the 2000's. Among those were: the '85 Harvest 50 at Stewart, Ohio in the TamRoy Mining race car; the '87 Dirt Race of Champions at Lancaster, South Carolina; the '91 Stick Elliot Memorial Race at Cherokee Speedway in Gaffney, South Carolina; the '92 STARS win at Parkerburg, West Virginia; and a '92 Hav-A-Tampa win at 311 Speedway in North Carolina. He continued to race dirt late models at Eldora and other tracks into the mid-2000's. He said, "I last raced dirt around 2004."

Rodney Combs was, without a doubt, one of the most consistent dirt late model drivers on Smawley's NDRA tour. One wonders how many more races and points titles he might have won, had he not been so dedicated to his racing career in Australia during those NDRA years. Something to think about.

Combs was inducted into the first class of the National Dirt Late Model Hall of Fame in 2001. Today, Rodney lives in Florida with his wife, Sue. They own and operate the American Diecast Company, which makes diecast replicas of race cars. I will always remember Rodney as one of the best dirt late model drivers that I had the pleasure to be around during the NDRA series.

Gary L. Parker

Jeff Purvis
NDRA Series Points Champion 1984 and 1985

Clarksville, Tennessee's Jeff Purvis was born on February 19, 1959. Jeff started racing at the age of 15, hence his #15. However, his career started to gain momentum in 1977. During this time he teamed with his father, Clyde, and began racing at his home track, the Clarksville Speedway. Purvis said he started winning so many races at the local speedway, "The race fans started booing me and throwing things at me." This was when he decided to take his dad's Imperial Motors sponsored race car on the road. This proved to be a good decision for him, but a bad decision for his racing competitors. Later, C.J. Rayburn offered Purvis a seat in one of his house cars. The Rayburn car was sponsored by Ray Baker Engineered Racing Engines, and Jackson, Tennessee's Wilkens Auto Sales.

Purvis had several big money wins all over the South, none bigger than the $50,000 NDRA win at the Hagerstown (MD) Speedway in June of 1983. This was the NDRA's biggest winner's purse at the time. In a thrilling finish, Jeff passed Freddy Smith with only five laps

Jack Purvis in the Imperial Motors/Baker Engines #15. Photo provided by Jeff Purvis.

Baker Blues in the News Congratulations

JEFF PURVIS

For Leading All 100 Laps and Winning the NDRA/Stroh's Race at Auto City Speedway in Flint, MI.

Jeff Has Won a Total of Five NDRA Races This Year Plus Finished Second in the Eldora World 100 — Out of Four Consecutive Years at the World 100 — Won Twice and Second Twice.

For "**Reliable Horsepower**" Call Us For **ALL** Your Engine Needs, From Parts to Complete Engines. Plus Used and Freshened Engines from 355 9-1 to 402 c.i.

We Have 15 Engines in Stock and Are Ready to Ship for Those End of the Year Big Money Races.

Baker Engineered Racing Engines
1422 Ironwood N.W., Grand Rapids, MI 49506
(616)677-5234

A Baker Race Engines ad from a racing newspaper. Ad provided by Jeff Purvis.

to go in winning the first annual Stroh's Free State Super National 100. They were followed by Larry Moore, Tom Peck, and Gary Stuhler in that order.

I first saw Purvis race in a Southern All Stars race at the Talladega (ALA) Short Track in 1983. He would go on to win the 50 lap event, during the series' inaugural season. Over the years, I watched him win races at a number of tracks throughout the South. One thing I always noticed about Jeff was his smooth, consistent style of driving. He never appeared to get rattled. This was perhaps the reason he collected almost 600 checkered flags during his long and successful

A promotional ad for the $50,000 to win Free State Stroh's Super National 100. Ad provided by Bob Markos.

career. Among those wins are: three World 100's ('83, '84, and '86), three National 100's ('82, '83, and '85), the 1986 Southern All Stars Series points championship, twelve NDRA series wins, and two NDRA points titles ('84 and '85).

Around 1985, Jeff's winning ways caught the eye of James Finch, owner of Lynn Haven, Florida's Phoenix Construction Company. Over the next 18 years, Purvis and Finch would go on to win hundreds of races together, including a number of STARS, NDRA, and other big money wins. Some of those big wins included: two North-South 100's ('87 and '89), several Hav-A-Tampa series wins, and three Hall of Fame 100's ('85, '86, and '87) at the famed Atomic Speedway in Knoxville, Tennessee.

However, his NDRA career is our focus here. Jeff started competing in the series in the early 80's. In two of his earliest series starts he finished

Lady Luck With Jeff Purvis in

By BRUCE GILLENWATER
Charlotte, NC

WOODSTOCK, GA (Oct. 7) — As only Lady Luck would have it. The same misfortune that kept him out of victory lane at the Smoky Mountain Invitational aided Jeff Purvis in capturing the sixth running of the NDRA/Stroh's Dodge Dixie Nationals at Dixie Speedway Sunday afternoon.

Purvis could do nothing but trail the speeding L.C. Smith Chevrolet/Tracer Jeans special piloted by Leon Sells, a local driver from nearby Mableton who led the first 90 laps. But a broken pinion gear shaft in the rearend sent Sells coasting into the pits, and this opened the door for Purvis. The Clarksville, TN, driver put his Imperial Motors/Wilkins Auto Sales/Carrera/Baker/Rayburn into the lead and, 10 laps later, crossed the stripe just ahead of Buck Simmons to win the one-week rain-delayed event.

"He (Sells) had the fastest car — he showed me that all day," said Purvis in victory lane. "I hate that

Jeff Purvis is in victory lane with Ms. Skoal Kimberly Gilmer (left) and Ms. NDRA Bobbi Byrd after winning the NDRA Dodge Dixie Nationals Sunday at Dixie Speedway. (Robert Turner photo)

Article on Purvis' Dodge Dixie nationals win at the Dixie Speedway. Article by Bruce Gillenwater provided by Jeff Purvis. (Continued on facing page.)

15th in the Buddy Hicks 100 at the Jackson (TN) Fairgrounds on August 8, 1980, a race won by Buck Simmons. The next night, August 9, Jeff finished 17th in the Joe Lunati Cams 100 at the Spencer Speedway in Tupelo, Mississippi, in a race that saw Larry Moore take the checkered flag. Like many of the NDRA drivers, Purvis began running the series for the large racing purses, and the national exposure the series brought to the drivers. He also felt the series brought a set of uniform racing rules (weight rules for cars) to the sport, making it fair for all the competitors. In addition, he saw the potential for growth the series had as it gained national sponsors such as, Schlitz Brewing Company, Stroh's Beer and the Chrysler Corporation.

In 1982, a young Purvis finished second to Larry Moore at the Dixie Nationals at the Dixie Speedway in Woodstock, Georgia. In a thrilling race, Purvis and Moore waged a race long battle that went down to the wire, with Moore winning by only a half car length at the finish

Dodge Dixie Nat'ls

he had the same bad luck I had two weeks ago. I was all set to take second place here — which at Dixie is like taking a win."

The feature failed to start on the first attempt when second-row starters Ronnie Johnson and Billy Clanton came together and knocked each other's handling out. Two attempts later the race got underway, and Sells had no trouble maintaining his lead — although Purvis was able to close to his rear bumper at times in lapped traffic.

"We worked so hard to get ready," stated Sells after parking his racer. "After getting so disgusted at Smoky Mountain, we were ready to do something here today. But I'd have rather had to go out on the first lap than to work as hard as we did and then lose it on the 90th."

Purvis had his own hands full in lapped traffic, as Simmons was able to close several times and, on lap 75, was able to pull even with him. But Simmons tagged a lapped car at this point, and the Baldwin driver lost his momentum.

"The slow cars just weren't getting out of the way," stated a disgruntled Simmons afterwards. "They stayed there all day — but not because the flagman was at fault. He was waving the move-over flag. I guess they should start black-flagging the idiots to get them to move."

Simmons' Carolina Tool/Barry Wright car had its own rearend problems, but during warm-ups Repairs were made just before the feature, including a transmission change.

Stan Massey, last year's winner made the most progress during the race. His Days Chevrolet-backed ride started 15th and steadily worked its way toward the front. But Ray Mason blew an engine on lap 59 while in fourth, and Massey could not avoid tagging the stalling car. Massey's front end was visibly knocked out of alignment but the NDRA regular was able to hold on to third place, despite a late race charge by track regular Ricky Williams.

(Continued on Page 25)

Article by Bruce Gillenwater provided by Jeff Purvis. (Continued from facing page.)

line. One of Jeff's first NDRA wins was the $50,000 Hagerstown win on June 11, 1983, mentioned earlier. He also won a series race at Atomic (TN) Speedway on August 27th of that same year. Purvis went on to finish fifth in the NDRA series points in '83, his first visit to the top five.

In 1984, Purvis started to dominate Robert Smawley's series, winning his first points title. During '84, Jeff scored five NDRA victory lane appearances out of the 16 series races. Those wins included two wins at the legendary Dixie Speedway in Woodstock, Georgia. He also won an NDRA race at a track known as the 81 Speedway in Wichita, Kansas on July 17. Jeff won the final two races of the season: on October 21, at Odessa Missouri's I-70 Speedway; and his last '84 win, at Cordele (GA) Motor Speedway on October 28th.

The beginning of the 1985 season saw Purvis continue to dominate the series. Jeff won three of the first five races that year. This included winning three races in a row. On April 13, he won at Spencer Speedway in Tupelo, Mississippi; April 20, he got the win at Atomic (TN) Speedway; and on May 11, he saw his third straight checkered flag at Tri-County Motor Speedway in Hudson, North Carolina. Throughout the year, things continued to go well for Purvis on the NDRA trail. He would go on to score two more wins in '85. His next to last win came at the Sharon Speedway in Hartford, Ohio. His final victory lane appearance was at the Auto City Speedway in Flint, Michigan on September 15, 1985. He finished the '85 season with five checkered flags.

Another driver who scored five series wins in '85 was, "Mr. Smooth," Billy Moyer out of Batesville, Arkansas. Moyer came on the NDRA scene with a bang in its final season. He finished tied for seventh on the all time series wins list with the Reading, Pennsylvania dirt star Kenny Brightbill, with five checkered flags each. However, Billy scored all his wins during the 85 season, winning five races in six starts, from June 16th until July 25th. This was probably the hottest win streak during the whole "Traveling Dirt Show" series. In addition, Moyer went on to finish second in what would be the last NDRA points battle in 1985.

Purvis went on to finish with 12 NDRA wins. This was good enough for fifth on the all time wins list, according to *Dirt on Dirt*. Jeff also won his second straight points title in 1985. However, this turned out to be the last points title for Smawley's NDRA series.

Billy Moyer's Larry Shaw #21 race car. He had all five of his NDRA wins in 1985, the last year of the series. Photo provided by dirtfans.com

Robert Smawley suddenly disbanded the series, and Purvis was never paid the $50,000 for winning the series' last points championship. It was a series that seemed to have everything going for it – national sponsors, the track owners support, driver support, and thousands of loyal race fans, but it was gone in an instant.

Even today, drivers and race fans alike wonder where the series would have gone, had it been operated in a more professional manner. After reading a March, 1988 article in STOCK CAR RACING by Dick Berggren, it appears Smawley just got burned out. Dealing with the drivers, track owners, the media, the rival STARS Racing Series, and especially the sponsors of his NDRA series; it all just got to him in the end. As Smawley said in the article, "I feel I just might have been ahead of my time." I recently spoke to Jeff, and he told me he harbors no ill feelings toward anyone in the series now. "All that's in the past," he said.

Purvis went on to win hundreds of races during the remainder of his racing career. Most of those dirt late model wins would be with his longtime sponsor, James Finch and his Phoenix Construction Company.

In 1989 Jeff made his NASCAR debut with Finch in the Busch Series (now the Xfinity Series). One year later, he made his NASCAR Cup Series debut. During Purvis' NASCAR career he drove cars for Bobby Allison, Joe Gibbs, Morgan-McClure, Richard Childress, and James Finch. However, Purvis enjoyed his best NASCAR success in the Xfinity Series. There he had four wins and 57 top tens in a 15 year career. Some of Jeff's other asphalt achievements include two Daytona ARCA 200 wins in '93 and '96, and the 1995 Snowball Derby winner.

Perhaps one of Purvis' best achievements was being inducted into the National Dirt Late Model Hall of Fame, in the Hall's inaugural class in 2001. This place of honor is where Jeff Purvis deserves to be. Few, if any, late model dirt warriors have accomplished what Jeff did on the red clay dirt tracks of our country. Purvis was one of the best in my book, and I have seen quite a few in the many years I have been following this sport.

The Rock-em, Sock-em, Travelin' Sideways Dirt Show

NDRA Top Five Point Standings by Year

1979
1. Leon Archer, Griffin, GA
2. Buck Simmons, Baldwin, GA
3. Bobby Thomas, Phenix City, ALA
4. Billy Thomas, Phenix City, ALA
5. Doug Kenimer, Dahlonega, GA

1980
1. Larry Moore, Dayton, Ohio
2. Rodney Combs, Lost Creek, WV
3. Jerry Inmon, Bruce, MS
4. Buck Simmons, Baldwin, GA
5. Don Hobbs, Bloomington, IND

1981
1. Buck Simmons, Baldwin, GA
2. Freddy Smith, Kings Mt., NC
3. Jerry Inmon, Bruce, MS
4. Larry Moore, Dayton, Ohio
5. Jack Boggs, Webbville, KY

1982
1. Mike Duvall, Gaffney, SC
2. Rodney Combs, Lost Creek, WV
3. Jack Boggs, Webbville, KY
4. Buck Simmons, Baldwin, GA
5. Larry Moore, Dayton, Ohio

1983
1. Rodney Combs, Lost Creek, WV
2. Freddy Smith, Kings Mt., NC
3. Larry Moore, Dayton, Ohio
4. Mike Duvall, Gaffney, SC
5. Jeff Purvis, Clarksville, TN

1984
1. Jeff Purvis, Clarksville, TN
2. Mike Duvall, Gaffney, SC
3. Jack Pennington, Winston, GA
4. Stan Massey, Mableton, GA
5. Jerry Inmon, Bruce, MS

1985
1. Jeff Purvis, Clarksville, TN
2. Billy Moyer, Batesville, ARK
3. Tommy Joe Pauschert, Carlisle, ARK
4. Jerry Inmon, Bruce, MS
5. Kenny Brightbill, Sinking Springs, PA

Chapter Five

Rising Stars on the NDRA Tour

This chapter takes a look at a few of the dirt late model drivers who became rising stars on the NDRA tour. Many of these drivers used this exposure to go on to long and successful careers in the world of dirt late model racing. Most of the attention will focus on the time they spent racing in Smawley's NDRA series, looking at some of the reasons why these drivers decided to compete in the nation's first national dirt late model racing series.

Ronnie Johnson

Right out of high school, Chattanooga, Tennessee's Ronnie Johnson knew exactly what he wanted to do for a living because –

A young Ronnie Johnson during the NDRA years. Photo from the Robert Smawley collection.

The Rock-em, Sock-em, Travelin' Sideways Dirt Show

he's doing it! Early in his racing career Johnson said, "Right now I love driving a race car; it's what pays the bills."

Ronnie was born on December 17, 1955 into a racing family, the son of the legendary Joe Lee Johnson, an early NASCAR star and winner of the 1960 World 600. Ronnie had a lot of regional racing success as an independent car owner and driver before deciding to give the NDRA series a shot. Most of the time he maintained as many as three race cars, setting each one up separately for different track conditions. Johnson recently told me in an interview for the book, RED CLAY AND DUST, "I like to run races as close to home as possible. If I can run for $3,000 or $5,000 close to home, then I stand a chance of clearing more money than if I ran for $10,000 several hundred miles away."

This was one of the reasons that Smawley's series was so appealing to him. Ronnie saw the large number of races in the series taking place in the East Tennessee area, at tracks like Atomic, Smokey Mountain, and Volunteer – tracks that he was already familiar with. That plus the announced $10,000 purses for a 100 lap event was enough to convince Johnson he needed to give the NDRA a try.

On October 26, 1979, Ronnie wrote his name in the NDRA record books. That day at the Volunteer Speedway in Bull's Gap, Tennessee, he won the NDRA Invitational Race of Champions, his first win on the tour. During his NDRA years, Ronnie drove some of the top race cars on the tour. As mentioned, he started out as an independent racer and car owner. He then drove for Darrell Monk Coal, Denny Ross and his WRC-built Camaro, and Bobby Paul and the #P1 pipe line race car. While driving the #P1 Bobby Paul car, Johnson added a series win, three second place finishes, and three track qualifying records to his credit.

Ronnie Johnson would continue to run a number of races on the NDRA tour throughout the mid-80's. His last series win came at one of his favorite tracks, Knoxville Tennessee's, Atomic Speedway on June 2, 1984.

After his NDRA years, Ronnie went on to win hundreds of races all over the country. In one of the few series he has competed for a points title, Johnson won three Southern All Stars Dirt Series Titles in "85, '87 and '88. However, two of his biggest wins came at the Dirt

Ronnie Johnson takes the NDRA win at Volunteer Speedway in Bull's Gap, Tennessee. Photo provided by Hugh Simpler.

Track World Championships ('92 and '94) at the legendary Pennsboro Speedway.

Johnson thought his career was nearing its twilight as the start of the 2000's began, sponsor money was drying up and super late model engines were getting too expensive to run. Then Mike Vaughn of Cartersville, Georgia introduced the Crate Racin' USA Series. This series, which became the NeSmith Dirt Late Model Series, perhaps saved Johnson's racing career. The series ran Crate CT 525 engines, costing a more affordable price of around $10,000 each. Since joining the series, Ronnie has won both the 2013 and '14 NeSmith Late Model Championships. He is also the series career wins leader with 25 victories. Today, Johnson is enjoying racing as much as ever. I don't see Ronnie Johnson retiring any time soon, not while he still enjoys winning races. And that is one thing he continues to do.

Ronnie was inducted into the National Dirt Late Model Hall of Fame in 2004; later, he was joined by Joe Lee and Jean Johnson, making it a family affair at the Hall.

The Rock-em, Sock-em, Travelin' Sideways Dirt Show

Jack Boggs

"Black" Jack Boggs was born in Webbville, Kentucky on April 4, 1950. He would go on to become one of the best "big money" race winners that dirt late model racing ever produced. If it was a high profile, big money race, put your money on "Black" Jack Boggs.

In 1980, Boggs picked up two major sponsors that would help put him on the road to national dirt late model stardom. First, he got Black Shamrock Coal Company's, Garland Flaugher on board. Then, Boggs was introduced to famed race car builder, C.J. Rayburn. The result was, the Flaugher/Rayburn race team with Jack Boggs as its driver.

Like so many other dirt late model drivers in the late 70's, Boggs had heard stories of a new dirt late model series that was being started by a Kingsport, Tennessee businessman by the name of Robert Smawley. The series was to be a national series called the NDRA, and it would pay $10,000 for a single 100 lap race. This was unheard of at the time, and Boggs wanted to learn more about the series. Because

Jack Boggs moments after winning the Super Bowl of Dirt" in the Pontiac Silverdome. Photo provided by Buddy and Cotton Duke.

Boggs scores another of his 1982 wins on the Schlitz/NDRA Pro National Series. This time at the Spencer Speedway. Photo provided by Buddy and Cotton Duke.

he, like so many other late model drivers, was tried of running for the small purses that most local tracks paid. So, at the last series race of the '80 season, held at the Volunteer Speedway in Bull's Gap Tennessee, Boggs decided to join the NDRA series, finishing 10th in that race.

In 1981 Jack would finish fifth in the NDRA Series points battle. He accomplished this without winning a single series race. However, his consistently high finishes would be good enough to earn him the '81 NDRA Rookie of the Year honors. Boggs would go on to be one of the top stars of the series in 1982. He started the season by winning one of the biggest and most unique races that any NDRA driver would compete in, the $50,000 "Super Bowl of Dirt Racing," held inside the Silverdome in Pontiac, Michigan on March 6, 1982, and witnessed by around 30,000 race fans. He went on to win the race on a rough, tiny quarter mile dirt track constructed inside the dome over fellow NDRA stars, Larry Moore and Freddy Smith. He proved that win was no fluke by winning the very next series event at the Metrolina Speedway in Charlotte, North Carolina on April 3, 1982.

Boggs had a breakout year in '82, winning four events. Out of the 25 NDRA races Jack ran in '82, he had fifteen top five finishes. In addition to his four checkered flags, he finished second once, third twice, fourth four times, and fifth four times. The two other '82 wins came on August 28th at the Spencer Speedway in Tupelo, Mississippi, and at the Cherokee Speedway in Gaffney, South Carolina on October 7, 1982. He finished a career high third in the "82 Series points, behind only Rodney Combs and the series winner that year, Mike Duvall.

The Kentucky driver also took home over $30,000 in winnings, not a bad year for a second year tour driver. This would be Boggs' best year in the NDRA. He never scored another win, or had another top five finish in the points chase during the remainder of the NDRA Series.

However, Boggs did go on to make a name for himself in the STARS Dirt Racing Series. His first STARS win came in 1984 at Log Cabin (VA) Raceway, and his last STARS checkered flag came at the Bluegrass Nationals at the Florence (KY) Speedway in 1997. In between these STARS wins he would go on to claim 25 others, finishing third on their all times wins list with 27 victories.

In some of the last races he ran, during Speedweeks 2000, competing in both STARS and UDTRA events, he drove his Rayburn house car to a fifth place finish in a STARS race. Unfortunately, on March 27, 2000 Jack Boggs was killed just nine days short of his 50th birthday. He will be missed by fellow drivers and race fan all over the country. "Black" Jack Boggs was a crowd favorite and will always be remembered for his "never give up attitude." Boggs was posthumously inducted into the inaugural class of the National Dirt Late Model Hall of Fame in 2001.

Donnie Moran

Frazeyburg Ohio's Donnie Moran came to the NDRA in 1982 with only three years of late model racing under his belt. The twenty year old driver was the youngest driver on the tour at the time. Rodney

20 year old Donnie Moran lifts the trophy after winning $35,000 at the Log Cabin Raceway. Photo from the Robert Smawley collection.

An overjoyed Moran celebrates with members of his pit crew. Photo from the Robert Smawley collection.

Combs had watched Moran from the start of his racing career and predicted a bright future for the young dirt star. Combs said, "It's unreal how he's come along the last couple of years." At the time Donnie was driving W.R.C. race cars that Combs built at the Dick

White, Mark Richards, and Rodney Combs racing facilities in Lost Creek, West Virginia. At the start of the '82 season Combs said, "He'll win an NDRA race very soon."

Rodney was right, Moran did win soon. However, he picked the biggest dirt race in history, up to that time, to score his first and (hard to believe) the only NDRA win of his career. On September 26, 1982, Donnie powered his #99 R&J Drilling/W.R.C. race car into the lead on lap 98 of the 100 lap NDRA/Schlitz Super Nationals. A crowd of 13,756 at Rocky Mount Virginia's, Log Cabin Raceway & Park stood on their feet for the final two lap dash to the checkered flag. Tom Laster, the "Okie from Muskogee," battled Moran to the finish line, finishing a close second. Laster was followed by Mike Duvall, Pat Patrick, and Pete Parker in that order. For his effort, the young Ohio dirt track ace won $35,000 of the record-shattering purse of $106,620 for the race.

Moran's consistent finishes, along with his big series win at Log Cabin earned him the NDRA Rookie of the Year Title for the '82 season. Donnie brought his young talent to the NDRA to gain some national exposure and for the large racing purses and sponsor incentives the series was paying out to its drivers. On both counts he came out a winner. First, he won the largest payout to a driver in dirt racing history (up to that time) $35,000. Secondly, the NDRA/Schlitz Super Nationals win, along with the '82 Rookie of the Year honors gave him the national exposure he needed to energize his racing career.

It would jump start a career that would take him to three All Star Circuit of Champions titles in '84, '85, and '86. He followed those titles with four STARS titles in, '91, '92, '95, and '99. The famed Eldora Speedway would be the site of Moran's most famous victory lane appearances. There he won four World 100's in, '89, '92, '96, and '97. Donnie also won the '96 Eldora Dream.

However, it was his $1 million dollar win in 2001 at a race known as the "Eldora Million," that would etch his name into dirt racing history. That day he pocketed a cool million dollars in his #99 race car and would forever be known in racing circles as, "Donnie Moran the Million Dollar Man."

Freddy Smith

The "Southern Gentleman," as Freddy Smith is known in the world of late model dirt racing, was born in Kings Mountain, North Carolina on December 22, 1946. Smith grew up around racing, his father Clarence "Grassy" Smith, building race engines since Freddy was a small boy. Later, Freddy, along with his brother, Buddy, and their father formed a family race team at their Smith and Sons Automotive race engine shop. As Freddy started to win late model races all over North and South Carolina, at tracks like Hudson North Carolina's, Starlite Speedway, and the Cherokee Speedway in Gaffney, South Carolina, the family race team started to focus solely on Freddy and his race cars.

Even in the late '70's, late model dirt racing was a hard business to make a living in. The Smiths once said, "We were like a lot of other teams at the time, just getting by." This was one of the biggest reasons the Smiths decided to run the new NDRA series. They had heard of the large winning purses being handed out on the tour. Also, they wanted to see if they could compete on the national level with all its dirt stars. After almost two years of competing on Smawley's dirt tour, Freddy was still without a win.

However, in 1980, all that was about to change. Smith would get his long awaited first NDRA win; he would then go on to win an unheard of, at the time, four more series checkered flags that season. Freddy scored his first '80 series win at Wythe Raceway in Wytheville, Virginia on May 31st. Toward the end of the '80 season Smith would go on a hot streak, winning four of the last six series races. The first time I saw "Fast Freddy," as I have always called him, was at the final NDRA race that season at the Volunteer Speedway at Bull's Gap, Tennessee on October 26, 1980. Smith was the hot driver for the season and was hoping to win the series' season finale. He did go on to win the race, his fifth of the season.

The '80 season turned out to be perhaps the turning point of Freddy's racing career. He caught the eye of Beady Lynch, owner of North Charleston, South Carolina's, B&D Industrial Boilers. Lynch bought Smith's race team and gave Freddy the major sponsorship he

Freddy Smith in the #00 racing with Buck Simmons in the Tri-City Aluminum #41. Photo provided by Jeff Smith.

needed to compete at the NDRA's national level. Fast Freddy would go on to win his last two career NDRA races in '85. Those wins came at the Kingsport (TN) Speedway on March 30th, and on June 1st at the Wilson (NC) Fairgrounds. After teaming with Lynch, Smith finished second twice in the series points chase, in '81 and again in '83. As a direct result of Smawley's series, Freddy gained national exposure and picked up a major sponsor in B&D Industrial Boilers. Smith finished sixth on the NDRA all time wins list with 9 victory lane appearances, according to *Dirt on Dirt*.

As a further result of the NDRA, Freddy went on to a become one of the best known and liked dirt late model drivers in the country over his long and successful racing career. He would go on to post 784 career wins. Some of his major victories include, three Blue/Gray 100's ('91, 2000, and '01) at one of his favorite tracks, Gaffney South Carolina's, Cherokee Speedway; five Dirt Track World Championships ('83, '85, '91, '93, and '98); two Hillbilly 100's ('81, and '83); and a two time winner of Eldora Speedway's "The Dream" ('94 and 2000). However, at the age of 61, Freddy was not through with major wins. On July 11, 2008, Smith scored his first Lucas Oil Late Model Dirt Series victory at the North Alabama Speedway in Tuscumbia, Alabama.

Freddy Smith in victory lane with Eva Taylor and Robert Smawley after winning his first career NDRA race a the Wythe Raceway on May 31, 1980. Photo from the Robert Smawley collection.

After a 48 year racing career, Smith drove his last race in the #00, hanging his helmet up for the last time in 2012. The "Southern Gentleman" was inducted into the National Dirt Late Model Hall of Fame in its inaugural class of 2001.

Chapter Six

The National Dirt Racing Association's Tour Busters

In the late 1970's, Robert Smawley's Winter's Performance Pro-National Series (NDRA) was gaining national attention from both race fans and drivers alike. The series was also acquiring a group of the nation's top late model drivers who became know as the "regulars" on the tour. Among them were Griffin Georgia's Leon Archer; Rodney Combs of Lost Creek, West Virginia; Baldwin, Georgia's Buck Simmons; Jerry Inmon of Bruce, Mississippi; and later, Larry Moore out of Dayton, Ohio; and Freddy Smith from King's Mountain, North Carolina to name a few. Some of these dirt stars would go on to become NDRA Series Points Champions.

However, as the series rolled into a number of tracks on the tour, many of the local Saturday night racers were lying in wait to try and take the spotlight away from the regulars on Smawley's "Traveling Dirt Show." This chapter takes a look at a few of what I call the "Tour Busters" of the NDRA.

H.E. Vineyard
1979 NDRA Looney Chevy 100 at Volunteer Speedway in Bull's Gap, Tennessee
June 9, 1979

Veteran dirt late model driver H.E. Vineyard had been winning races at Volunteer and other East Tennessee dirt tracks for years. He had out dueled some of the best drivers the area had to offer such as, "Little" Bill Corum, Melvin Corum, "Big" Bill Corum, L.D. Ottinger, Buddy Rogers, and Herman Goddard to name but a few. However, Vineyard's driving skills would be put to the test, as the dirt stars of the NDRA were about to invade one of Vineyard's "home turfs," the Volunteer Speedway in Bull's Gap, Tennessee. It was June 9, 1979 and it was the next to last NDRA race of the inaugural '79 season.

H.E. Vineyard powers through a turn at the Volunteer Speedway at Bull's Gap, TN. Photo provided by David "Peanut" Jenkins.

Qualifying had just ended and Baldwin Georgia's Buck Simmons had won the pole for the race with a time of 15.57. Along side him was the "Southern Gentleman," Freddy Smith, who qualified just a tick slower at 15.58. The night's NDRA racing format was slightly altered for the race. Normally only the top three fast times are locked in. However, this night the first seven were given a free pass to the feature. Vineyard turned a 15.97 and had to run a heat race to earn a spot in the 100 lap main event. He easily won his heat race and started in the fifth row.

As the green flag waved, Smith in the #00 took the lead from Simmons. On lap 21, Simmons went underneath Smith and took the lead in heavy lapped traffic. Vineyard didn't start making his move until around lap 25. He was still in the ninth position, but started to pick off some of the elite NDRA drivers one by one. By lap 40, Vineyard was in fifth position, and the crowd came to its feet each time he picked up a position. On lap 41 he made his boldest move of the race to that point, passing the number 3 and 4 cars coming out of the fourth turn. Vineyard held the number three spot until lap 75. On lap 76 he was under Tom Helfrich and was in second place. Heading toward lap 80, Vineyard was quickly making his way toward the leader Simmons. Around lap 88 he caught Buck and the battle was on. From that point on the fans, in the packed bleachers, were on their feet. For several laps, Vineyard and Simmons changed the lead several times to the delight of the big crowd.

With one lap to go, the white flag came out. Simmons was able to move up along side Vineyard in turns one and two. Vineyard, who was not going to be denied this night, pulled in front of Buck going down the back straight-a-way. Simmons made one final attempt to get under Vineyard in turns three and four, getting almost side by side as they came to the finish. In the end, as the two crossed the finish line, Vineyard won by less than a half a car length. This was one of the best races the series had enjoyed up to this time.

Newspaper article by Wayne Phillips about the Vineyard NDRA win at Volunteer Speedway. Photo provided by David "Peanut" Jenkins.

For this night at least, H.E. Vineyard proved he could run with the best dirt late model drivers the nation had to offer. He took his red #24 to victory lane that night and went home with the $10,000 winner's share. He had out dueled Simmons and a field of dirt late model stars that included, Tom Helfrich, Snooks Defoor, Bud Lunsford, Rodney Combs, C.L. Pritchett, Doug Kenimer, and a number of others.

The Looney 100 started 28 cars that night. The top 10 in order were, H.E. Vineyard, Buck Simmons, Steve Smith, Tom Helfrich, Snooks Defoor, Fulmer Lance, Rodney Combs, Charles Hughes, Bud Lunsford, and Doug Kenimer.

Vineyard would go on to win hundreds of races all over the South during his career. He won many of those, driving for Bob Miller in the '80's. I had the good fortune to be part of his pit crew during the Bob Miller era, when he drove the white #3 Hawkeye Trucking/Miller Bros. Construction Co. race car to so many wins. He would later come close to another "tour buster" win at Atomic Speedway on November 8th of '81, finishing second to "Little" Bill Corum, who was another NDRA "tour buster" on that day. Like him or not, H.E .Vineyard was one of the best dirt late model drivers the South has ever produced. He was inducted into the National Dirt Late Model Hall of Fame in 2007.

Bud Lunsford

1980 NDRA Spring Nationals at Rome Speedway in Rome, Georgia April 20, 1980

Born in White County, Georgia in 1935, Gainesville Georgia's Bud Lunsford won an amazing 1139 races during his 25 year racing career, winning over 600 races in dirt late models. Bud recently told me, "I had T-shirts printed after I won, what I thought would be my last race, number 1138. However, I was at Toccoa Speedway one night and decided to run one more race at the track where I scored my first victory." He went on to say with a laugh, "And wouldn't you know it, I won number 1139. I never had anymore T-shirts printed with the 1139 wins on them."

Bud would go on to race about every type of race car that had four wheels, including, flat head jalopies, modifieds, super modifieds,

Bud Lunsford celebrates Rome NDRA win with Robert Smawley, and Donna Fox. Photo from the Robert Smawley collection.

skeeters, and dirt late models. Lunsford was one of those Southern dirt late model drivers that won races all over the South. Around 1971 Bud won an amazing 63 feature races. This was followed up the next year with 64 checkered flags. Lunsford told me, "That amount of wins was possible at the time because most of the drivers were racing four and even five times a week." He, along with drivers like Charlie Mincey, Leon Sells, Buck Simmons, Leon Archer, Jody Ridley, and Doug Kenimer were almost taken for granted, as just the norm, by the race fans all over the metro Atlanta area. This all changed as Robert Smawley's NDRA burst on the scene in 1978. It didn't take the new national touring series long to figure out, "The good ole Southern boys were going to be hard to out run."

In addition to being a legendary dirt racer, Lunsford was also an innovative chassis designer and builder. He was perhaps the first driver in Georgia to use an "in-box" transmission, like those used in sprint cars. He also was a master at making his late model dirt cars lighter and lighter. We won't go into some of the ways he was able to accomplish that here. Let's just say he was probably one of the drivers

The Rock-em, Sock-em, Travelin' Sideways Dirt Show

that caused weight rules for race cars to be implemented by a lot of race tracks.

Bud was no stranger to winning at the half-mile Georgia red clay track known as the Rome Speedway. He is the all time wins leader at Rome with 97 victory lane appearances. So it came as no surprise to many, including myself, that on April 20, 1980, Bud Lunsford or "Bud L," as he was known by the local race fans and drivers alike, would go on to become another of what I call a tour buster on the NDRA traveling dirt series.

Lunsford had already registered an NDRA win on October 28, 1979, at a track he helped design and build, the Dixie Speedway in Woodstock, Georgia. So as the NDRA series rolled into Rome in the Spring of 1980, Lunsford was feeling confident about his chances of a second series win in the Metro Atlanta area. He was never one who liked to travel long distances to race. So the fact that the NDRA had scheduled races for both, Dixie and the Rome Speedways was very much to his liking. At Dixie, Bud had driven his familiar gold and black #49 Camaro to the series win. Bud told me in a recent interview, "The biggest help I received in the Dixie NDRA win was when the Hoosier Tire Rep, Doug Sopha, provided me with a set of Hoosier asphalt racing slicks, that probably won that race for me." He went on to say, "When I put those slicks on I thought my race car was on rails, it ran so good."

The NDRA/Spring Nationals was a two day event that opened the 1980 racing season for the legendary Southern promoter Mickey Swims', Rome Speedway. Friday night saw a very fast qualifying session, with rising NDRA star, King's Mountain North Carolina's Freddy Smith, setting a new track record of 15.63 on his way to pole position for Saturday's main event.

As mentioned earlier, Lunsford was always making changes and fine tuning his race cars. So after a poor qualifying session, Bud, driving the black #49 Russell Lee owned race car, took it to his shop that Friday night to make some changes to it for the next day's race. Bud told me, "Russell and his crew were not too happy with me changing the car." He said, "Those ill feelings continued on race day, as I was having a tuff time getting the car to handle." Bud went on, "The car

Lunsford in the Russell Lee's black #49 passes Don Hobbs on his way to his second NDRA win, this one at Rome. Photo provided by Jeff Smith collection.

continued to perform poorly in the heat race, and I started around 22nd spot in the next to last row."

However, Bud Lunsford was about to prove all his doubters wrong. It was while I was writing the book, RED CLAY AND DUST, that I got a very accurate account of the Lunsford win at Rome that day. It came from another NDRA driver, "Little" Bill Corum, who fell out of the race due to a wreck during a heat race. Corum then became a spectator and my "eye witness" for a very good description of the race.

"Little" Bill said, "Bud was having a bad day and had to start the 100 lap event in 22th position or so." He continued, "As the race went green, Lunsford lost a couple more positions. But after about 10 or so laps Bud started to pick off race cars at a pretty fast clip." Corum then said, "I turned to my wife, who was sitting on the race trailer beside me, and said 'I can tell you who will win this race.' She said, 'Who?' And I said, 'Bud Lunsford'."

Corum's wife then said, "No way, not with all these good drivers."

During the next 20 laps or so, Corum said, "Bud was passing cars about one or two a lap, passing Johnson [Ronnie], Archer [Leon], Hobbs [Don], and several others." He continued, "Close to the half way mark he passed Duvall [Mike], Thomas [Bobby] and some others. The track was a two groove track that day, and Lunsford started using

The Rock-em, Sock-em, Travelin' Sideways Dirt Show

the high groove to his advantage, blasting by car after car." He said, "The final 20 laps saw him go under Mincey [Charlie], Moore [Larry], and then go by Sells [Leon], then Osteen [Doug] and the pole sitter, Smith [Freddy] over the next 15 or so laps."

Corum went on to recount, "He continued to run down the leader, Rodney Combs, who continued to run the low groove." Then Little Bill said, "With about four or five laps to go, you could see that Lunsford was going to catch him before the race ended." At that point Corum told of the finish, "As the white flag came out, Bud caught Combs going into one and two; they swapped the lead down the back straight-a-way. Then going through turns three and four they were almost side by side. Combs continued to run low and Bud was in the high groove." Corum said finally, "As they went under the checkered flag, Lunsford held on in the high groove and won the race in a very close finish." Freddy Smith, who set a new track qualifying record of 15.63, started from the pole. Smith led the early laps and finished third. He was followed by Doug Osteen, and Leon Sells.

After Lunsford's win that day, Bobby Paul, owner of Larry Moore's #P1 pipe line car, protested the tires Lunsford used in the race. Paul claimed the tires had no serial number on them and were experimental tires, not legal for the race. Robert Smawley then used a chalky substance to show the serial number had been there but was rubbed off. Since it could not be proved that it did not happen during the race, the protest was not upheld and Lunsford was declared the winner. I asked Bud about the tires recently and he said, "The tires did have a serial number on them. They must have gotten rubbed of during the race. As far as I know anyone could have used the tires that I ran that day."

Bud Lunsford scored two victories on Smawley's NDRA tour, both at local tracks that were right in the Gainsville, Georgia driver's "backyard." Bud would go on to win many more dirt late model races during his career. He told me recently that he last drove competitively in 1987. He was rightfully inducted into the National Dirt Late Model Hall of Fame in 2003. After seeing Bud recently at his family owned bowling lanes in Gainsville, I believe he could still give the "good ole boys" a run for their money in a black and gold #49.

Gary L. Parker

Stan Massey

1981 NDRA Schlitz Nationals 100 at Dixie Speedway in Woodstock, Georgia
October 4, 1981

Stan Massey grew up around dirt racing, so it was only natural that he would become one of what is known in racing circles as a "weekend warrior." Stan's dad, Ed Massey, was a car owner for years for Stan's uncle, the legendary National Hall of Fame late model driver, Leon Sells. Young Massey proved that racing was truly in his blood when he scored his first win at Senoia Raceway on July 14, 1972. Over a racing career that saw him win around 200 races, Stan celebrated his last career checkered flag at Seven Flags Speedway (the old West Atlanta Raceway) on June 17, 2000.

In between he would dominate late model dirt racing at legendary Southern race promoter Mickey Swims', Dixie Speedway. Massey has won more late model dirt races at Dixie than anyone, with 69 confirmed wins. Along the way, he also won four dirt late model track championships at the famed speedway in Woodstock Georgia. However, it is the 1981 NDRA Schlitz Nationals 100, held at Dixie Speedway, that is our focus here.

Stan Massey takes a victory lap after winning the '81 NDRA/Schlitz Nationals 100 at Dixie Speedway. Photo provided by Jeff Smith collection.

The Rock-em, Sock-em, Travelin' Sideways Dirt Show

Massey receives a victory kiss from Miss NDRA, Eva Taylor, as happy race fans look on. Photo provided by Jeff Smith collection.

It was early October at the 3/8-mile red clay oval known as Dixie Speedway. Robert Smawley's NDRA series was in town for the big $17,000 to win three day show. Most of the stars of the touring series were on hand, with the exception of Rodney Combs who was racing in Australia, as he had done for a number of years. However, his ugly green #16 Howe Camaro was at Dixie being driven by none other than Ed Howe himself.

Massey had been the hot driver at Dixie recently, winning six of the last eight races. Still with 61 cars, most of them NDRA regulars trying to qualify for the race, Stan was considered a "dark horse" at best. Someone forgot to tell Massey that, as he qualified third fastest on the field. The only drivers faster were, fellow Georgia driver Buck Simmons in second, and pole sitter, Freddy Smith with a fast time of 16.44. Sponsors had put up prize money for the top three qualifiers, Smith received $2400, Simmons got $500, and Massey took home $300 for his effort.

It had been a busy weekend at Dixie with a total of six heat races being run on Saturday night to set the field for the two NDRA races to be held on Sunday. As racing began before a packed house on Sun-

The ugly green #16 Howe car. Ed Howe finished second behind Stan Massey in this car. Photo provided by Jeff Smith collection.

day, the 50 lap consolation race was won by Strasburg Ohio's Brad Malcuit. This set the stage for the 100 lap rumble on the hard Georgia red clay.

The start of the 100 lap feature saw pole sitter Freddy Smith jump into the lead, followed closely by Simmons and Massey. On lap 13, Massey passed Simmons and set his sites on the leader Smith. Right before the quarter race mark at lap 24, Stan powered under the #00 of "Fast" Freddy Smith to take the lead. From that point on, Massey maintained the lead.

Five caution flags came out during the 100 lap event bunching up the field behind Massey. However, he had little trouble pulling away each time the green came out. One of the fastest cars of the day was South Carolina's Mike Duvall, who made a crowd pleasing run from the 16th starting spot to move into the second spot, after Simmons engine blew on lap 75. Duvall would go on to experience problems of his own; a leaking tire left the door open for Ed Howe to pass him and finish in the runner-up spot.

Howe in that ugly green #16 asphalt car was, next to Massey's win, the surprise of the race. Driving in only his third race of the year, Howe started in 12th position and moved steadily through the star studded field to finish second 1.3 seconds behind Stan the man in his familiar #22 machine.

Tires played a big part in this daytime race, Massey no doubt made the right tire choice. Car owner Jack Diemer chose to use a hard Firestone tire for the dry slick hard red clay of Dixie. The top 10 on that October 4th Sunday in order of finish were: Stan Massey, Ed Howe, Mike Duvall, Larry Moore, Bud Lunsford, Mike Head, Brad Malcuit (the consolation winner), Leon Sells, Freddy Smith, and Charles Hughes.

This was by far, the biggest win of the Mableton, Georgia drivers career. Massey was joined in victory lane by an overjoyed crowd of local race fans. The $17,000 was also the largest payday of Stan's career. Runner up Ed Howe received $5,000 for his runner up finish in that ugly green car.

Stan Massey later proved his win was no fluke. Almost two years to the day, on October 2, 1983, Massey won his second and last NDRA race at, you guessed it, the Dixie Speedway.

The start of the '81 NDRA/Schlitz Nationals 100 at Dixie Speedway. Photo provided by Jeff Smith collection.

Gary L. Parker

"Little" Bill Corum

1981 NDRA Lunati Cams 100 at
Atomic Speedway in Knoxville, Tennessee
November 8, 1981

"Little" Bill Corum was a member of the legendary racing Corum family out of Maynardville, Tennessee. He was a dominant force in late model dirt racing in the East Tennessee area for a number of years. Corum won hundreds of races all over the Knoxville, Tennessee area and throughout the Southeast, at tracks that included, Tazewell (TN) Speedway, Smoky Mountain Raceway, Volunteer Speedway, and at one of his favorite tracks, the famed Atomic (TN) Speedway.

"Little" Bill Corum at Atomic Speedway. Photo provided by "Little" Bill Corum.

So, to no one's surprise, "Little" Bill, along with several other local favorites like Herman Goddard, Buddy Rogers, Tootle Estes, and H.E. Vineyard, felt they had a real shot at a win at the ultra fast Atomic Speedway in the late fall of '81. Vineyard had already scored an NDRA win at the Volunteer Speedway in nearby Bull's Gap, Tennessee in the late Spring of '79. In addition, Corum had recently enjoyed a good outing at an NDRA race at the Wytheville Raceway in Wytheville, Virginia, winning pit steward "Fuzzy" Orange's "Hot Dog" award for an outstanding race and a third place finish. So all these local drivers knew a win was certainly possible at Atomic.

The Atomic Speedway had always been known for its quick lap times, and on this day it would prove no different. After a delay due to rainy weather, Ohio's Larry Moore sat on the pole with a fast time of 12.53. Rodney Combs had been quick too, but after the weather delay he had other commitments and could not make it back for the race. Combs, who was friends with H.E. Vineyard at the time, decided to have Mark Richards, who was part of the Combs racing team, bring the car back to Atomic and have Vineyard drive it in the race. According to Vineyard, he was told by Rodney to, "Drive the car like it was yours." Because of an NDRA rule on driver changes, Vineyard had to start in the rear with the white and red #5 J.D. Stacy sponsored race car.

In addition to "Little" Bill Corum and Larry Moore, there were several other fast cars in the race that day. There was Chattanooga driver, Ronnie Johnson, who always seemed to run well at Atomic; long time Newport, Tennessee veteran, L.D. Ottinger; and Gaffney, South Carolina dirt star, Mike Duvall in his "Flintstone Flyer" race car.

However, this day would prove to be the driver from Maynardville Tennessee's day to become an NDRA "Tour Buster." The three fastest cars on the day proved to be, "Little" Bill, Mike Duvall, and the surprise of the day, H.E. Vineyard in Rodney Combs' car. The race was a battle, all day, between Duvall and Corum. It seemed the two stayed glued to each other throughout the entire race. As the 100 lap race progressed, Vineyard, in the Combs #5, passed car after car to the delight of the overflow crowd. He moved steadily through the field, passing stars like Ronnie Johnson, Dale McDowell, Sherman Howell, Jack Trammell, Herman Goddard, and Luther Carter on his way toward Duvall and Corum.

As Duvall and "Little" Bill battled for the lead, they were almost unaware of how fast Vineyard was gaining on them. As the laps ran down it would soon become a three car battle for the lead. With about 10 laps to go, the crowd was about to witness a battle to the finish. The last few laps saw Duvall hold onto the lead, with Corum

H.E. Vineyard stands beside the #5 Combs car he drove to a second place finish in the Lunati Cams 100 at Atomic Speedway. Photo provided by David "Peanut" Jenkins.

and Vineyard, in a back and forth war for the number two spot. Some have said, Vineyard passed Corum only to have the caution flag come out, thus H.E. had to restart behind him. Either way, it was a battle to the checkered flag for, it appeared, the runner-up spot to the "Flintstone Flyer."

After the race, Duvall, in the winning car, was weighed by NDRA officials and found to be "light" at the scales. He was disqualified and the win went to "Little" Bill Corum, in the Bud Mullins/Stars and Stripes #21. Vineyard, who came from the rear of the field in the Combs car, finished second, followed by Joe Richey, L.D. Ottinger, Johnny Williams, Buddy Rogers, Jerry Inmon, Jack Trammell, Sherman Howell, and rounding out the top 10, Rick Rogers.

Corum takes his victory lap in the #21 after winning the Lunati Cams 100 at Atomic Speedway. Photo provided by "Little" Bill Corum.

Corum told me recently, "That was probably my biggest win of my racing career. I know it was one of the most exciting wins, because it was an NDRA win on one of my favorite tracks." Later, driving for Butch Curtis for a number of races, "Little" Bill recently told me, "I had a number of classic battles with racing legend, Scott Bloomquist in the Curtis car at Atomic Speedway."

By his account, Corum won almost 400 feature races during his racing career. He also won several late model track championships at Atomic Speedway, Volunteer Speedway, Tazewell Speedway, and the Newport Speedway. "Little" Bill told me his last late model dirt race was at the Smoky Mountain Speedway during the 1992 season. If you ever see my racing friend, "Little" Bill Corum, at the Tazewell Speedway, stop and talk racing with him, you will be glad you did.

In the series' almost eight year run, these were but a few of the many local dirt late model drivers that became "Tour Busters" on Robert Smawley's national dirt racing tour. Many of these drivers used their NDRA tour buster wins as a spring board to gaining much needed sponsorship and help in furthering their racing careers.

Chapter Seven

Robert Being Robert

There will never be another Robert Wayne Smawley. According to longtime friends, Johnny Robinson, Buddy Duke, and Michael "Cotton" Duke, "They broke the mold when Robert came into the world." The friends continued, "Robert was a guy who could find humor in just about everything that was around him. He was the best I ever saw at putting together and playing practical jokes." They concluded by saying, "Nothing or nobody was off limits to Robert."

I had the pleasure of meeting and talking to Smawley quite a bit during the NDRA series. For sure, he was perhaps one of the best promoter/showman to come along in the last hundred years, ranking right up there with P.T Barnum and others. You could tell he enjoyed being the center of attention at his NDRA races, always dressed in his signature "checkered flag shirt," or one of his ruffled shirts, and of course, those white trousers (white trousers at a dirt race, oh well). Finally, he wore enough jewelry to be a walking advertisement for Jared's Galleria of Fine Jewelry. At times I believe he thought he was going to be the next Elvis.

Buddy Duke told me someone once. Quoting someone, he said, "The best way to describe Robert was, he was a cross between Elvis Presley and Jim Jones." However, Buddy could not for the life of him remember who said it.

But don't let Smawley's style of dress fool you. Robert Smawley was what I'll call "a visionary businessman, organizer, and promoter who was simply years ahead of his time." However, as we will see in the following pages, he was a man who loved having fun with everyone and everything around him, and he certainly enjoyed life to its fullest.

Smawley appeared born to be a promoter. He just had the natural ability to excite people including the series sponsors, the fans, the track owners, and especially the drivers. He built up his events, making them exciting, fun, and always "going" to be spectacular,

Robert, enjoying some kisses from his trophy queens before an NDRA race. Photo from the Robert Smawley collection.

constantly changing promotions for both fans and drivers. Heck, after listening to one of his pre-race buildups you felt you had to be there to see as they say, "What was going to happen next."

Almost to a man, all the series drivers liked Smawley. After all he had brought late model dirt racing into the national spotlight, and at the same time, he made it profitable for both the drivers and car owners. But Robert was still Robert; you never knew what to expect. Just ask drivers like C.L. Pritchett.

Smawley had an uncanny ability to get out of many a tight situation. Both Buddy and Cotton Duke told me about a funny situation that happened one time in July of 1983 at an NDRA race in Odessa, Missouri at the I-70 Speedway won by Tom Helfrich.

Smawley in his famous white pants and checkered flag shirt. Photo from the Robert Smawley collection.

The series rules stated that if drivers were involved in an racing accident, all cars had to go to the rear of the field, no matter who caused the accident. That night a local favorite was involved in an accident, while running up front. The wreck was no fault of his, but to the disapproval of the local crowd, he was put in the rear of the field. The crowd became very disruptive throwing things onto the track. At the end of the race it became a mob scene, according to the Dukes. They said Smawley ordered all his staff into the scoring tower, and track officials had to call the police to try and restore order.

The crowd was becoming more hostile toward Smawley and his crew, some even shouting to, "Burn the scoring tower down."

The Rock-em, Sock-em, Travelin' Sideways Dirt Show

The Dukes said, "We had all the money for the night's event in a large duffle bag and Cotton asked Robert, 'What are we going to do?'"

They went on to say, "Robert in his usual calm manner told Cotton to take his NDRA shirt off. Cotton took the shirt off, standing there in his t-shirt, jeans, and tennis shoes. All of the sudden Robert told him, 'Wipe your hands on the dirty floor and rub your face and shirt with the dirty mess.' At that point, Cotton looked like he was just another dirty pit crew member. Smawley told him, 'Take the duffle bag with the money and walk calmly down the steps.'

"As Cotton opened the door to leave he asked Robert, 'What do I do when I get to the bottom of the steps?'

"Robert, in his never get excited manner, said, 'Run Damn it!'"

After the police came, order was restored and Robert and his staff were able to leave and go back to their motel. This was just one of the many situations that Robert got himself, and sometimes his staff, out of. He had an ability to quickly read a situation and come up with a quick solution.

Driver C.L. Pritchett gets an unexpected kiss from Smawley. Photo from the Robert Smawley collection.

As I said, no one, and I mean no one, was off limits to Smawley and his antics. In Larry Moore's fine book, ON TOP OF THE WORLD, Moore tells of a story where Robert tried to call the Queen of England to have her talk to his NDRA Champion, Leon Archer.

Larry said, "We got rained out at Golden Isles Speedway in Brunswick, Georgia, So everyone went Robert's motel suite to (you know) have some fun." Moore then said, "As the night wore on Robert had one of his crazy ideas." Larry continued, "Smawley said he had the phone number to Queen Elizabeth and was going to call her and have her talk to his champion, Leon Archer." Larry with a laugh went on, "We all thought this was bull; nobody calls the Queen of England."

Moore said, "I listened in on an extension in the next room as Robert made a call, and someone with a British accent said, 'Who is calling?'

"Robert then said, 'It's Robert Smawley of the NDRA in America calling the Queen.' However, Smawley had forgot about the time difference," Moore continued.

"After a few minutes someone came back to the phone and said the Queen had retired for the night."

Larry then said with a big laugh, "Robert then said, 'Well wake the (blank) up. I know she will want to talk to our NDRA Champion.'" In closing Moore said, "When Robert said that the phone went, 'CLICK.' I guess the British were not yet ready for Smawley's brand of humor."

Robert's staff was always fair game to a lot of his practical jokes during the series. Robert's Secretary, Connie Noel Melton, told me about a joke Robert played on her while preparing for the race at the Silverdome in February of '82.

She said, "I was down on the floor of the Silverdome watching the workers, who were putting the dirt down for the race track." She said, "All of the sudden a young fan appeared, asking excitedly for my autograph." Connie continued, "I began to wonder how this young fan even knew I was with the series, let alone, why they were wanting to get my autograph." She then said, "I thought about it for a moment and then I said, 'Robert has got to be behind this'." Connie concluded with a big grin, "As I looked around to see if I could find Robert, I hap-

The Rock-em, Sock-em, Travelin' Sideways Dirt Show

pened to look up at the press box, and there he was laughing, that darn Robert."

Many a car owner and a lot of drivers fell victim to Robert and his constant practical jokes. For example, he would have the front desk make wake up calls at 3 a.m. for some of the car owners and drivers, just to have a big laugh the next morning. On one occasion he canceled the room reservations for Jerry Inmon's car owner, Dick Stevens. When Stevens showed up for his room he was told by the front desk that his room had been canceled and had already been given to someone else. When Stevens showed up at the track that night he said,

Robert clowning around with one of his staff members at the motel after an NDRA race. Photo from the Robert Smawley collection.

"I saw Smawley coming toward me almost bent over with laughter." Stevens said, "I knew then it was that damn Smawley that had canceled my room reservations."

One of the best examples of Robert just being Robert was at the '82 NDRA Awards Banquet in Daytona Beach, Florida. Again, it was Connie Melton who told me this story.

She said, "It was the Year Mike Duvall had won the points title. Most of the sponsors had brought their clothing lines to the banquet and wanted Robert to provide models to present their products to those in attendance that night.

Robert Smawley hosting the 1982 NDRA Awards Banquet in Daytona Beach, Florida. It would get a little wild later. Photo from the Robert Smawley collection.

Connie said, "True to form Robert goes out onto the streets and gathers up, not professional models, but 'professionals' of another trade and brings them to me to model the clothes." Connie continued, "By this time it was to late to get real models, so I had to use these 'Ladies' to model the clothes. Some of them were 'feeling no pains' as they modeled the clothing lines, to the delight of most of the sponsors." Melton finished by saying, "Most of those in attendance that night were more interested in getting with the 'models' than they were the clothing lines."

NDRA staff members, Tim Taylor, Cotton Duke and Johnny Robinson, having a little pre-race fun with a pretty young fan. Photo from the Robert Smawley collection.

According to Buddy Duke, Robert, his staff, the drivers and car owners were always taking every opportunity to have a good time (And I mean a good time.) Buddy told me one of the funniest stories I ever heard about some of Robert's antics. Duke said, "It all started after a rain out at Dixie Speedway in Woodstock, Georgia. About everybody connected with the series was staying at the Holiday Inn in nearby Marietta, Georgia." According to Duke, "The motel was perhaps the finest in the area at that time, complete with a big fountain with humanlike statues at the front entrance." Buddy said, "As the Night wore on, many in the group were starting to get out of hand with their mischief (We cannot talk about a lot of it here). This included Robert who, in the wee hours of the morning, was swimming in his 'birthday suit' in the pool."

Buddy said, "By this time the management was tired of all the complaints that were pouring in so they called the police." He continued, "Of course when they arrived everyone vanished from site, including the nude Robert." Buddy then said, "Since Smawley was pretty much in charge of the group, the police were looking for him. They looked all over for him, covering the whole area several times." Buddy was laughing as he said, "They never found Robert, but they walked by him several times." Duke closed with a big grin on his face by saying, "Robert had been in the fountain all that time posing as a nude statue."

Robert's staff, including Buddy and Cotton Duke, Johnny Robinson, Tim Taylor, and others all enjoyed their time with the series. Most

Robert and Tom Sefickes celebrating Smawley's first national sponsorship with the Schlitz Brewing Company. Photo from Robert Smawley's family album.

said, "It was always laid back, no matter if you were at dinner, the motel, or at the track; everyone had a good time, all the time."

Finally, Robert was a master at getting the most from his sponsors. Starting with the Winter's Performance sponsorship, to the first national dirt racing sponsorship with Tom Sefickes and the Schlitz brewing company, the $500,000 Dutch Treats partnership, to finally, the million dollar Stroh's deal, Robert always knew how to come up with the money to run his Pro National Series.

One of the funniest sponsor stories had to do with Robert picking up the Stroh's sponsorship in 1983. Both Buddy and Cotton Duke told me this story. Recently, Buddy Duke went into detail about it by saying, "At the last minute I had to go with Robert to the corporate offices of Stroh Brewery Company in Detroit." Buddy said, "We left in such a hurry that I basically just jumped into the car and we left." Duke said, "Someone had to go along just to be sure Robert would show up in time for his meeting at Stroh's." Buddy continued, "As we were driving toward Detroit, the always thinking Robert looked over at me and said, 'Did you bring a suit?'

"I said, 'Of course I didn't bring a suit.'

"Robert then said, 'Damn,' and he stopped and bought me a suit. Later out of the blue Robert said, 'Do you have a brief case?'

"I answered, 'Of course not, Robert. Why would I have a brief case?'

"Robert said, 'Damn'."

So, according to Duke, "We stopped at a K-Mart, and he bought me a briefcase."

"After arriving early for their meeting, we were taken upstairs to the board room, that included a very long meeting table. Since none of the Stroh's people had arrived Robert told me, 'Buddy, you go and sit at that end of the table. if I ask you a question you open the briefcase (which of course had nothing in it) and act like you are looking at some papers. In a minute or so I'll ask you about something, and you say, 'You have got that exactly right, Robert.'

Buddy said, "Thankfully as the presentation was given by Robert, no questions were asked of me." Duke said, "Smawley gave such a

Robert and Leon Archer share some fun with a pile of money. This was just Robert being Robert. Photo from the Robert Smawley collection.

good presentation, which included a professionally done video of the 1982 NDRA Metrolina Speedway race, that the Stroh's people wanted us to come back at 3 p.m. and present the proposal to their boss. Robert agreed and we came back at three. Robert was asking for what he thought was a large amount, $150,000. So, in true Robert form he gave the presentation again."

Duke continued, "After the presentation, all the members of the Stroh's team left the room for about 10 minutes. When they came back they asked Robert if he would mind coming back at 6 p.m., because they wanted the owner of the company, Peter Stroh, to make the final decision."

Buddy then said, "Well old Robert, showed his salesmanship by giving his best presentation yet to Peter Stroh. Duke concluded by saying, "After hearing Robert's proposal, Peter Stroh picked up the phone and told his secretary to make out a check for not a $150,000, not even $500,000, but for a cool one million dollars." According to Buddy Duke, "Old Robert had done the selling job of his life."

Duke said the Stroh's sponsorship included, $500,000 for the points fund and the Stroh's Winner's Circle program, $250,000 for the program and staff, $250,000 for marketing, and two Stroh's show cars complete with staff. The Stroh's deal was announced to the public by NDRA President Robert Smawley and John MacLeod, spokesman for the brewery, before the start of the '83 NDRA season.

As you have seen, Smawley was a "one of a kind" in the world of promoting, salesmanship, and visionary planning, but most of all, he was the "King" of practical jokes and "good times." He was, "Just Robert being Robert."

Gary L. Parker

Chapter Eight

Some Milestone Races of the NDRA

We now take a look at some NDRA races that became, what I'll call milestone races on Robert Smawley's late model "Traveling Dirt Show" tour. These races were either unique, one of a kind races, or paid the largest series racing purses at the time. Each of these races played an important part to the history of the NDRA, and the significance each race played to the series will be examined.

The MRE Eastern Classic
Rolling Wheels Raceway Park

The NDRA/MRE Eastern Classic was held on October 8-10, 1980 at the famed Rolling Wheels Raceway Park, located in Elbridge, New York. The race was significant to the history of the NDRA because it was the first time that a major dirt late model event was part of the almost week long DIRT car Modified annual events at the track.

It was Ed Howe, the Beaverton, Michigan racing chassis guru who pointed both Rodney Combs and Larry Moore toward Rolling Wheels because of the big money purses being paid there. He told them it was a modified race, but with some modifications they could run the race. It was the 1979 race and both Combs and Moore made the show after making changes to their cars that included, removing the spoilers, raising the roofs of the cars, and a few other changes. However, the Howe cars would experience engine problems during the practice rounds keeping both drivers out of the main event.

It was a very cold day at Rolling Wheels Raceway Park for the Schlitz/Pro National series, MRE Eastern Classic. Rodney Combs and Larry Moore hoped to make a better showing for the first NDRA sanctioned event at the famed 5/8 mile dirt track. The 1980 season was winding down and Combs and Moore had been battling for the series points championship all year. Rodney had set a new track record for the race and was starting on the pole.

The Rock-em, Sock-em, Travelin' Sideways Dirt Show

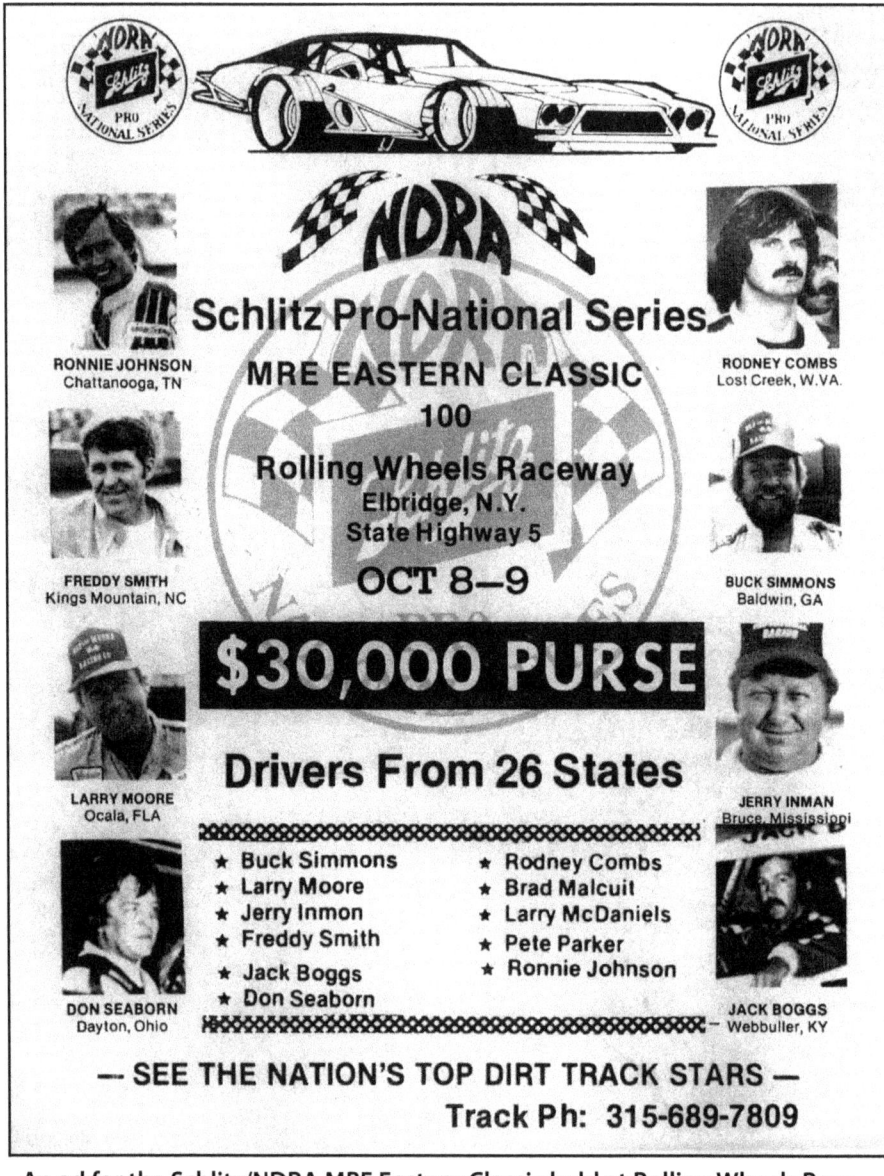

An ad for the Schlitz/NDRA MRE Eastern Classic held at Rolling Wheels Raceway. Ad provided by Bob Markos.

    Combs would cruise to victory in his #5 Tri-City Aluminum Camaro, Claiming $5,000 of the $30,000 purse that Day. Rodney enjoyed good luck that day compared to a number of other NDRA regulars. Jerry Inmon, who always seemed to have bad luck when leading a

Ad for the "Super Bowl of Dirt" held in the Pontiac Silverdome. Ad provided by Bob Markos.

race, stayed true to form. After passing Combs for his first NDRA race lead, during the middle stages of the race, Jerry hit an axle from another race car. The axle knocked a hole in both his radiator and oil pan forcing Inmon to the pits, ending his chances for a win.

Even the series points leader, Larry Moore, didn't finish the race because of an oil pump failure. He had been running a solid second to Combs before going out on lap 78.

As the race wound down the temperatures dropped into the low 20's, and the frigid weather cracked the plastic front spoilers on a number of the race cars. However, Rodney was able to endure the cold temperatures and claimed the checkered flag over second place Freddy Smith in the B&D Industrial Boilers #00 Camaro. The rest of the top 10 in order were, Will Cagle, David Hess, Buck

The Rock-em, Sock-em, Travelin' Sideways Dirt Show

Simmons (in the other Tri-City race car), Gerald Chamberlain, Kenny Brightbill, Skip Furlow, Tom Peck, and Jack Pennington in tenth.

There would be another NDRA race at Rolling Hills in 1981, with Larry Moore taking the win in that race. These two races, held in conjunction with the DIRT car modified events, would help Robert Smawley's NDRA receive a lot of national exposure in the Northeast.

The Super Bowl of Dirt
Pontiac Silverdome

This was probably the most unique race that the drivers of the NDRA ran during the series' almost eight year run. A crew of about 25 workers spent five intense days forming a tiny quarter-mile dirt race track inside the Pontiac Silverdome out of 6,000 yards of mother earth.

The indoor racing event was organized and promoted by a group known as American Productions, under the watchful eye of promoters, Joe Zimmerman and Jeff Pierce. It did have NDRA sanction, although

NDRA Drivers and workers look over the construction of the track inside the Silverdome. Photo from the Robert Smawley collection.

Robert talks to one of the American Productions staff standing on the Silverdome dirt track. Photo from the Robert Smawley collection.

A look at the track and crowded infield before the start of the "Super Bowl of Dirt" race. Photo from the Robert Smawley collection.

The Rock-em, Sock-em, Travelin' Sideways Dirt Show

An ad for the "Heroes vs. Outlaws" All Star Race, held in the afternoon before the "Super Bowl of Dirt" race. Ad provided by Bob Markos.

Robert Smawley had little to do with the event, other than advising the promoters and bringing a lot of his series drivers.

It was March 6, 1982 and about 30,000 race fans were awaiting the start of the 50-lap Budweiser Super Bowl of Dirt. The race had the distinction of being the first time full-bodied race cars had raced

Jack Boggs in the #B4 takes the checkered flag in the "Super Bowl of Dirt".
Photo from the Robert Smawley collection.

Tight racing by a pack of cars during the famed Silverdome race. Photo from the Robert Smawley collection.

indoors. The consolation races were over and Tony Izzo and Doug Kenimer had recorded wins, and were preparing to compete in the 50 lap main event. Fast qualifier for the race was Georgia's Buck Simmons with a time of 13.50.

In addition to the 50 lap late model event, a 35-lap "Heroes versus Outlaws" race, featuring CART, NASCAR, USAC, ASA, and NDRA stars, like David Pearson, Buddy Baker, Neil Bonnett, Kyle Petty, Ken Schrader, Tom Sneva, Johnny Parsons, Jr., Bob Senneker, and others was held in the afternoon.

Hometown favorite, Joy Fair won the star studded event. It was a surprise win for Fair because it was the first time he had ever raced on dirt. David Pearson, who competed in the entire racing program, saved face for the pros, by finishing second. He was followed by Indy car driver, Johnny Parsons, Jr. in third. Attendance wise, the afternoon affair was not the success the promoters had hoped for, but the evening's main event would more than make up for it.

"Black" Jack Boggs was a driver you could always put your money on in a "big" money race. Boggs, fresh off his 1981 NDRA/Schlitz Rookie of the Year season, started on the pole and led the 50 lap Budweiser Super Bowl of Dirt flag to flag. Jack, driving the #B-4 Flaugher Coal Camaro, used skillful passing in traffic to keep Larry Moore's Firebird behind him for the entire race.

The first 15 laps of the race saw several caution flags keep the field tightly bunched on the tiny indoor dirt oval. As the flagman signaled the half way mark, Larry Moore continued to ride nose to tail with Boggs. They were followed by Don Seaborn, Ron Hekkema, and Ken Schrader. Georgia's, Doug Kenimer was able to work his way from 14th all the way to third before fading back and settling for a sixth place finish. NASCAR star, David Pearson, finished in 15th position, leaving the race after only completing 20 laps.

As the race was nearing the 40 lap mark, the third and fourth place cars of Johnny Parsons, Jr. and Ken Schrader tangled in turn two, putting both drivers out of the race. In one of the last moves

Jack Boggs, along with his wife, are all smiles after his big win in the Pontiac Silverdome. Photo from the Robert Smawley collection.

of the race, Freddy Smith moved past Hekkema's Gaerte Engines Camaro to take third. Following Boggs, Moore, Smith, and Hekkema to the finish line were Charlie Swartz, Doug Kenimer, Buck Simmons, Ed Sanger, Ray Godsey, and Don Seaborn in tenth place.

Boggs was all smiles in victory lane as he pocketed $8,000 of the $50,000 Super Bowl of Dirt purse. Jack said the track was "rough" but he was able to move through traffic and maintain his groove by being in the lead.

American Productions had been talking about an encore Super Bowl of Dirt in 1983. However, as some of the driver's checks turned out to be bad, the promoters never carried through with another event. American Productions claimed that all the expenses involved with the races had bankrupted the group. Several drivers filed a class action lawsuit, but no one who filed every received any money. It was a sad ending to what could have been perhaps an annual dirt racing event.

The start of the historic race at Log Cabin Raceway on September 24, 1982. Photo from the Robert Smawley collection.

Donnie Moran's crew changes his tire and sends him out for the eventual win in the Log Cabin race. Photo from the Robert Smawley collection.

Gary L. Parker

The 1982 NDRA/Schlitz Super Nationals 100 Log Cabin Raceway

On September 24, 1982 Donnie Moran, the 20 year old dirt sensation from Frazeyburg, Ohio, over came a flat tire with 31 laps to go and won the '82 NDRA/Schlitz Super National 100 at Rocky Mount Virginia's, Log Cabin Raceway. This was, at the time, the largest purse ever paid out for an NDRA race. Also, the 13,756 race fans who witnessed the race were the largest crowd to watch a late model dirt race at the time.

In a recent interview, Buddy Duke told me an interesting story about the historic Log Cabin race. He said, "At the Log Cabin Race, I was in charge of ticket sales at the main ticket booth at the track." Buddy continued, "I could not take the money fast enough because the fans were in such a hurry to get in and find a good seat. They were actually throwing the money at me as they went by." Duke said, "There was so much money, I was actually standing in money in the booth and it was up to my knees, really! He concluded by saying, "I had never seen so much money. Robert's staff would come by every so often and stuff money in pillow cases and take it away." The Race paid a record purse (at the time) of $106,620 of which Donnie Moran took home a record $35,000 payday for his win.

The race was a caution flag nightmare. There were a total of 20 caution flags, 14 of those were for right rear tire failure, including one with 31 laps to go for the eventual winner, Donnie Moran. Most of the top contenders were forced to make stops to replace blown right rear tires. They included, Rodney Combs, Charlie Swartz, Jeff Purvis, Mike Duvall, and even eventual second place finisher, Tom Laster.

The race appeared to be lost for young Moran, after his right rear went flat with only 31 laps remaining. However, as other drivers started to experience the same fate, Donnie moved steadily through cars, and as a caution came out on lap 79, he found himself in fifth position. Moran began believing he might have a chance for the win after a caution put him behind Duvall.

The latter part of the race witnessed a hard fought battle between Rodney Combs, in his J.D. Stacy #5 Firebird, and Moran in his

R&J Drilling race car. The battle raged from lap 91 until Combs had a flat with only a couple of laps remaining. With two laps remaining, the big crowd was on its feet for the sprint to the finish between Tom Laster, the "Okie from Muskogee" and young Moran. The white flag came out and the battle was on. Moran crossed the finish line 1.1 seconds ahead of Laster. Finishing behind the front duo were Mike Duvall, Pat Patrick, and Pete Parker. Another fast car that day was pole winner, Jim Curry, who led the first 82 laps of the race, but he was not there at the end.

In victory lane Moran was all smiles as he said, "Rodney was guarding the low groove when we were racing for the lead. That might have been a factor with his tires, because when you keep it low, tires spin. Wears them out."

In an interesting note, Donnie Moran won the biggest winner's purse for an NDRA race at the time, $35,000. Surprisingly, it would be his one and only NDRA checkered flag.

Twenty year old Donnie Moran in the winner's circle after winning the $35,000 check from Smawley, holding the checkered flag. Photo from the Robert Smawley collection.

Gary L. Parker

1983 First Annual NDRA/Stroh's Free State Super National 100
Hagerstown (MD) Speedway

An ad for the Free State Stroh's Super National 100. Ad provided by Bob Markos.

On June 11, 1983, the NDRA/Stroh's Free State Super National 100 paid the largest winner's purse in NDRA series history. Jeff Purvis would pass King's Mountain, North Carolina's, Freddy Smith with only five Laps to go to claim the $50,000 winner's check. Purvis won the race "the hard way," coming from the back of the pack all the way to the front. Only one lap had been completed when Purvis was involved in an accident with third place starter, John Mason. Purvis pitted the #15 under caution and changed the flat left rear tire.

Jeff returned to the race in the rear of the 32 car field, and his work was cut out for him. The battle at the front was between Tom Peck, the pole sitter Charlie Swartz, and Freddy Smith. However, Purvis was moving toward the front like a runaway freight train. By lap 29 he was already in the sixth position. Jeff was running fourth only five laps later. Swartz had been the early

Jeff Purvis in Hagerstown victory lane holding the $50,000 winner's check and the checkered flag. Photo from the Robert Smawley collection.

leader, but on lap 34 Smith passed Swartz for the lead, while Purvis moved into third.

At the half way mandatory fuel stop, the running order was, Smith, Purvis, Peck, Larry Moore, and Donnie Moran. After the restart, Smith was able to keep Purvis behind him, while Moore continued to stay within striking distance in third. With about 25 laps to go the battle for the lead began to intensify, with Jeff now challenging Smith for the lead on almost every lap.

The stage was set for a thrilling finish, when a caution came out with only nine laps remaining. The flagman gave the green with just five more circuits remaining. Smith was running the high groove and Purvis was able to use the low groove in battling Smith for the lead. The big crowd was on their feet as the two dirt warriors staged a side by side battle for the lead. It was going to be Jeff's night to shine, as

Jeff Purvis before an NDRA race during driver introductions. Photo provided by Jeff Purvis.

he made a clean pass on Smith and took the lead and the win. Some have called it the $40,000 pass. That was the difference in the $50,000 Purvis won versus the $10,000 Smith got for finishing second. Moore, in an ill handling car, finished third followed by Tom Peck, and Gary Stuhler in fifth.

The NDRA/Stroh's Free State Super National 100 race was significant for two important reasons. First, as mentioned earlier, it was the biggest winner's purse ($50,000) in Smawley's series history. Secondly, Purvis' biggest career win brought him into the national spotlight. It was the springboard that launched his rise in the NDRA, leading to his back to back series point's titles in '84 and '85.

After his big $50,000 win at Hagerstown, Jeff would become the dominant force in Smawley's series for the last two years of "The Traveling Dirt Show," recording 10 checkered flags over the final two years, according to *Dirt on Dirt*.

The 2nd Annual 1985 NDRA/Stroh's Invitational New Kingsport (TN) Speedway

An ad for the Second Annual Stroh's Invitational held at the New Kingsport Speedway. Ad provided by Bob Markos.

On October 13, 1985, Georgia's Buck Simmons would win the NDRA/Stroh's Invitational and a total of $30,000 in winnings. No one knew at the time, that this race would be the last big money event of Robert Smawley's historic dirt late model national series.

Buck Simmons took the green flag on the start of the NDRA/Stroh's Invitational and lead the entire 100 lap event. But according to Buck, "I was under pressure from the first lap to the last lap, more pressure the last 10." That pretty much summed up the event. After the 24 starters completed the first lap without a caution, something that had not been done the whole night, the top 10 settled in for the first half of the race. The top 10 were, Simmons, followed by Tommy Joe Pauschert, Larry Phillips, Willy Kraft, Jeff Purvis, Billy Moyer, Bob Pierce, Freddy Smith, Leon Sells, and Scott Bloomquist.

The second half of the race saw Simmons and Pauschert open up about a two-second lead over the third and fourth place cars of, Kraft and Purvis. Around lap 72, it appeared

A newspaper article by Nelson Redd on Buck Simmon's win in the $250,000 Stroh's Invitational. Article provided by Bob Markos.

Pauschert was going to make a move to pass Buck, but a caution ended that threat. Pauschert said, "That Caution helped Buck and probably won him the race."

According to Simmons, the last 10 laps were tightly contested, with Simmons taking the checkered flag for the $20,000 win over, Pauschert, Purvis, Smith, Bloomquist, Pierce, Sells, Phillips, Brightbill, and Stan Massey rounding out the top 10.

Buck won the Dutch Treats fast qualifier award the night before, over Tommy Joe Pauschert, and about 140 other drivers. In doing so he received and extra $10,000 from one of Robert Smawley's newest series sponsors, the Dutch Treats Cigar Company. The cigar company had recently added a $500,000 package to the NDRA series. In addition, Buck represented the I-85 Speedway in Greer, South Carolina. His win in the Kingport invitational also secured that track a $30,000 point fund from the Stroh Brewery Company, the major sponsor of the event.

Simmons drove a two year old Barry Wright chassis with a new rear suspension system to the big win. Buck took a total of $30,000 in winnings back to his home in Baldwin, Georgia in what he called, "A helluva day." Little did anyone know at the time, this would be the last big money event for the NDRA. The series ran only two more races after the Kingsport event; the last NDRA race was at Tri-County Speedway in Hudson, North Carolina, won by Kenny Brightbill on November 16, 1985.

Chapter Nine
Reasons Behind the Sudden Demise of the NDRA

This chapter takes a look at some of the many reasons put forth over the last thirty years, as to what caused the sudden demise to the nation's first national dirt late model racing series. We will take a look at a number of these, ranging from race track instability, to dealing with promoter support and cooperation, a lack of driver support and unity, the racing news media's lack of coverage or sometimes its negative coverage, and the rise of Carl Short's STARS Series are some of the reasons mentioned. These ideas along with a number of others have been put forth in the years since the NDRA abruptly ended after the 1985 season. As we examine a number of these scenarios, I will also put forth another little know reason that could have played a part in Robert Smawley's decision to suddenly end the, "Biggest Show in Dirt Racing."

As early as the second NDRA race in August of 1978, we see the beginnings of track promoters wanting to retract or change their dealings with Smawley and his NDRA series. For example, Edgar "Hard Rock" Gault, the promoter of Cherokee Speedway in Gaffney, South Carolina, was given the choice by Smawley of either taking a percentage of the gate admissions or renting the track to the NDRA for three days. Gault chose the rental option. However, after Gault saw the amount of money he had lost by his decision, he became bitter and looked for ways to try and make the series and its owner, Robert Smawley, look like the bad guys. According to Buddy Duke and others who were there at the time, the crowd was so large that certain parts of the stands actually collapsed as a result of the weight. Gault wanted to use this to try and gain back some of the money he felt he had "lost." Even after Smawley repaired the stands the next week with money out of his own pocket, Gault continued to complain about the series and how he was "done wrong" by the NDRA. He vowed never to have the NDRA back. It was only after David and Deborah Perry took over as promoters, that the series was brought back. That was in October of 1982 in the series' final appearance at the track; that race was won by Kentucky's Jack Boggs.

NDRA Moves to New Offices; Releases Schedule

KINGSPORT, TN — The National Dirt Racing Association has moved into new offices which will house the sanctioning body's national headquarters and softwear concessions operation, according to NDRA president Robert Smawley.

NDRA's new address is 102 Post Oak Drive, Kingsport, TN 37663. Because the location is in a different telephone exchange area, the sanctioning body's phone number has been changed to (615) 239-3554.

The staff remains virtually intact, including Donna Tranbarger, executive secretary; Denise Lorenzo, secretary and mail clerk; and Helen Williams, accountant. Lyndia Frazier has joined NDRA as news media coordinator and writer.

"The move into the new offices was made out of consideration for its larger capacity," Smawley said. "The new office is complete with advertising layout facilities, mass mailing equipment, word processors and computers. The new office complex will definitely enable the NDRA staff to service sanctioned tracks, sponsors and the media better in the future."

Smawley also announced he is vigorously pursuing national sponsorship for the NDRA programs to fill the void left by Stroh's decision to end its involvement in all forms of auto racing. He recently attended a sponsorship seminar in Chicago and indicated he should have a sponsorship announcement forthcoming in about 30 days.

National Dirt Racing Association 1986 Schedule

Date	Track	Location
May 9,10	Senoia Raceway	Senoia, GA
May 23,24	Crossville Raceway	Crossville, TN
Jun. 6,7	Lancaster Speedway	Lancaster, SC
Jun. 13	North Mississippi Speedbowl	Byhalia, MS
Jun. 14	Spencer Speedway	Spencer, MS
Jul. 4-6	**Firecracker NDRA Nationals** West Virginia Motor Speedway	Mineral Wells, WV
Jul. 11,12	I-30 Speedway	Little Rock, AR
Jul. 14	Fun Valley Speedway	Hutchinson, KS
Jul. 15,16	Eighty-One Speedway	Wichita, KS
Jul. 19,20	I-70 Speedway	Odessa, MO
Jul. 23	Monett Speedway	Monett, MO
Jul. 25,26	I-44 Speedway	Lebanon, MO
Aug. 8,9	Sharon Speedway	Hartford, OH
Aug. 22,23	Tentative	
Aug. 29,30	Six-Cylinder World Championship Lancaster Speedway	Lancaster, SC
Sep. 12	Smoky Mountain Raceway	Maryville, TN
Sep. 13	Atomic Speedway	Knoxville, TN
Oct. 2-5	**NDRA $¼ Million Invitational** I-70 Speedway	Odessa, MO
Oct. 17,18	Senoia Raceway	Senoia, GA
Oct. 24,25	Lanier Raceway	Gainesville, GA

super **RACING** — Winston Racing Series

Hickory Speedway
Hickory, NC

Every **Saturday Night**

According to Hoosier Tire Representative Doug Sopha and others, this type of treatment of the NDRA series went on throughout much of its almost eight year run. Doug said, "Robert had a set way of running his events, and some, not all, of the promoters or track owners, would make changes before or after the races had started." He went on to say, "A lot of the appeared disorganization and sudden changes to an event were brought about by many of the owners and/or promoters and in some cases were not Robert's fault." Sopha finished by saying, "This was just one in a series reasons for Robert ending the series, he just got tired of dealing with a number track's that refused to cooperate and help make the series a professionally run success that it could have been."

A number of tracks saw the success the NDRA had at their facilities and tried to do their own version of an NDRA event. Smawley said, "Tracks like Log Cabin Raceway and Park where I had one of my most successful races, the $35,000 to win event in '82, tried to run the event by themselves the following year and failed to pull it off without me." Smawley went on to say, "Most promoters had no idea of what was involved in pulling off an event the size of the Log Cabin race or how to sell it to the fans and drivers. They failed to see that there was an art to such things as, sponsors, advertising, promoting, and other hidden things involved in making a big race a success."

Many tracks had very good success with their NDRA races. Tracks like Atomic (TN) Speedway, and Mickey Swims' two Georgia tracks, the Dixie and Rome Speedways, enjoyed a number of great years with the NDRA. Most of the tracks that enjoyed a great association with Smawley left the NDRA events almost entirely to Robert and his staff to promote and run.

Another area mentioned quite often had to do with Smawley's dealings with the drivers. Not all, but many, had what I'll call the "Saturday Night Racer Mentality." That is thinking only of themselves, and not about the NDRA and its long range benefit to the drivers and their future. In the beginning, most of the drivers racing the series wanted it to become a success. However, as the series continued, some drivers started demanding more and more from Smawley and the NDRA, while giving less and less of themselves to the series and its sponsors.

Smawley once used a photo of star driver Jeff Purvis to prove a point. He said, "Is there anything in that picture (Purvis wearing nothing that promoted an NDRA sponsor) that would make a sponsor like Stroh's Beer want to spend a half million dollars on a series." Smawley knew the importance of sponsors to his series and wanted those sponsor's decals and patches used on his driver's racing suits and cars to promote their products. Doug Sopha said, "Most drivers complied with Robert's wishes, but some like Jeff and a few others balked at the idea." In any sport, a sponsor wants to see his or her name as often as possible. Imagine if the winning driver in a Nextel Cup event failed to acknowledge the sponsor, such as by not wearing the Nextel race cap. Where would that series be?

An often mentioned issue having to do with the drivers, was their loyalty to the NDRA series. Smawley wanted to be able to assure race fans that certain drivers were going to be at his events when they came to town. Sopha said, "If you advertised that six star drivers were going to be at an event, and only three of them showed up it made Robert and the whole series look bad in the eyes of race

STARS - SHORT TRACK AUTO RACING SERIES

1984 - STARS race results:

Date	Track	Laps	Winner
June 9	Hagerstown Speedway, Md.	100 L	Rodney Franklin
June 23	Log Cabin Raceway, Va.	100 L	Jack Boggs
July 1	Brownstown Speedway, Ind.	50 L	Jeff Purvis
July 7	Muskingum Co. Speedway, Ohio	50 L	Freddy Smith
July 8	Pennsboro Speedway, W.V.	50 L	Freddy Smith
Aug. 10	Wayne County Speedway, Ohio	50 L	Ray Godsey
Aug. 18	Brownstown Speedway, Ind.	100 L	Kenny Simpson
Aug. 24	Hagerstown Speedway, Md.	75 L	Rodney Franklin
Aug. 25	Hagerstown Speedway, Md.	100 L	Bobby Wearing
Sept. 2	Pennsboro Speedway, W.V.	100 L	Larry Moore
Sept. 22	311 Motor Speedway, N.C.	100 L	Rodney Franklin
Oct. 6	Wayne County Speedway, Ohio	100 L	Skip Furlow
Oct. 7	Winchester Speedway, Va.	100 L	Jack Boggs
Oct. 14	Hagerstown Speedway, Md.	150 L	Jack Boggs
Oct. 21	Pennsboro Speedway, W.V.	100 L	Jack Boggs

1984 - STARS final points:

1.	John Mason	1829
2.	Larry Moore	1740
3.	Jack Boggs	1707
4.	Rodney Franklin	1373
5.	Denny Chamberlain	1307
6.	Bobby Wearing	1285
7.	Rodney Combs	1199
8.	Noel Witcher	1186
9.	Russ Petro	1140
10.	Freddy Smith	1091

Racin' JOHN MASON - Bob Appleget pic

fans." This was perhaps one of the biggest reason for his insistence upon drivers signing a contract in order to be eligible for the series points fund. The final year saw Smawley give all drivers a contract to sign. He was later asked, How many drivers returned signed contracts? "Not one of them signed them," he said. He was asked why? Robert replied, "It's the racer mentality. They were more interested in going Saturday night racing, they don't give a damn about the NDRA, its sponsors, or the growth of the sport." Many including, Buddy and Cotton Duke, and Doug Sopha have said this was just another in a long line of reasons why Smawley just got fed up with the series and all it's problems.

Also, Smawley felt he didn't receive a fair shake from the news media. In one of his most damning indictments of the racing media, Robert became furious over a Dick Berggren article in STOCK CAR RACING magazine entitled, "The Rise & Fall of the NDRA," because it failed to have his major sponsor, Stroh's Brewery, in the article's title. He said, "Get Stroh's Beer in the title. Racing owes a lot to Stroh's Brewery." This was perhaps the biggest example of the media's failure to recognize Robert's series sponsors. Again, can you imagine at the time if the racing media had just called it the "NASCAR Cup Series," instead of the NASCAR Winston Cup Series. Smawley just wanted fair coverage for his sponsors, like NASCAR was getting. Can you really fault him for that?

In another example of not getting fair media coverage, CIRCLE TRACK MAGAZINE failed to provide any coverage of the '85 Stroh's/NDRA Invitational held at Kingsport. This was dirt racing's biggest purse at the time, but was not worthy of any coverage in CIRCLE TRACK. Really!

According to Smawley, an event was sometimes given negative coverage or some elements of a race were exaggerated or misrepresented. Robert said a classic example of this was an article on the 1985 Stroh's $250,000 Invitational, held at Kingport, Tennessee. In the article, author David Allio called it, "The Quarter Million Dollar Dust Bowl." Robert countered the article by saying, "There wasn't any more dust at that race than you'd ever see at any afternoon dirt track race." My wife and I were at that race and I tend to agree with Smawley about the dust situation that day. I have seen a lot more dust at a daytime race on many occasions than I saw that day (Several races at the legendary Lakewood Speedway in the late 70's come to mind), and I have been going to dirt track races for well over fifty years. This type of media coverage was just another example of a long list of problems that the NDRA and Smawley had to deal with during most of the series' history.

Over the years a number of people have said that October 13, 1985 was the day that Robert Smawley's NDRA died. That was the day the NDRA/Stroh's Invitational was held in Smawley's hometown of Kingsport, Tennessee. This was a $250,000 event (biggest ever at

STARS - SHORT TRACK AUTO RACING SERIES

1985 - STARS race results:

Date	Track	Laps	Winner
Feb. 12	Volusia County Speedway, Fla.	30 L	Billy Moyer, Jr.
Feb. 13	Volusia County Speedway, Fla.	30 L	Jeff Purvis
Feb. 14	Volusia County Speedway, Fla.	30 L	Freddy Smith
Feb. 15	Volusia County Speedway, Fla.	30 L	Larry Phillips
Feb. 16	Volusia County Speedway, Fla.	50 L	Larry Moore
April 28	Hagerstown Raceway, Md.	75 L	Rodney Franklin
May 18	Brownstown Speedway, Ind.	100 L	Dusty Chapman
May 25	Speedway 7, Ohio	50 L	Don Gross
May 26	Buckeye Speedway, Ohio	100 L	Jack Boggs
June 1	Southern Ohio Raceway	40 L	Jack Boggs
June 9	Hagerstown Speedway, Md.	100 L	Rodney Franklin
June 19	Clearfield Speedway, Penn.	40 L	Jack Boggs
June 23	Muskingum Co. Speedway, Ohio	40 L	Larry Moore
June 30	Brownstown Speedway, Ind.	100 L	Billy Moyer, Jr.
July 4	Florence Speedway, Ky.	50 L	Jack Boggs
July 6	Southern Ohio Raceway	50 L	Charlie Swartz
July 7	Pennsboro Speedway, W.V.	50 L	Jeff Purvis
July 13	Pennsylvania Motor Speedway	40 L	Jack Boggs
July 20	Hagerstown Speedway, Md.	100 L	Rodney Franklin
July 27	Pennsylvania Motor Speedway	40 L	John Mason
July 28	West Virginia Motor Speedway	50 L	Jack Boggs
Aug. 10	Florence Speedway, KY	100 L	John Mason
Aug. 17	Brownstown Speedway, Ind.	100 L	Kenny Brightbill
Aug. 31	Buckeye Speedway, Ohio	100 L	Larry Moore
Sept. 1	West Virginia Motor Speedway	100 L	Jack Boggs
Sep. 14	Hagerstown Speedway, Md.	85 L	Buddy Armel
Oct. 6	Winchester Speedway, Va.	200 L	Jeff Purvis
Oct. 13	Hagerstown Speedway, Md.	150 L	Rodney Franklin
Oct. 27	Pennsboro Speedway, W.V.	100 L	Freddy Smith

the time), and little did anyone know, this would be the series' last big extravaganza. The NDRA had only two more breathes of life remaining after Kingsport, those being: a race at Peach State Speedway in Jefferson, Georgia, and the final race held at Tri-County Motor Speedway in Hudson, North Carolina on November 16, 1985, won by Kenny Brightbill.

Over the last thirty years, the half filled stands at Kingport have been cited many times as the series' "death blow." Some have even said this started sponsors to think about abandoning the NDRA and Robert Smawley. However, the race was an exciting one, with eventual winner, pole sitter Buck Simmons being pressured on almost every lap of the 100 lap event. Smawley insisted he had the funding from a number sponsors to have another season in '86. He said the funding was there from Stroh's for 1986 if he had wanted it. In February of '85 Consolidated Cigar had joined the series with its Dutch Treats brand to the tune of $500,000 for three years. He also said that he had been approached by Coors Beer. The beer company's interest in the NDRA stemmed from Tom Siefkes, the Eastern Sale Manager of Coors at the time. He was a long time friend of Smawley's, and the person who brought Robert his first national sponsor, the Schlitz Brewing Company deal in 1980 when he was working at Schlitz. Robert even mentioned Hoosier Tire as another possible national sponsor option.

Robert insisted that major sponsors were, "Not interested in crowds in the grandstands." He said, "They were interested more in product and product placement." Smawley went on to say that even without a national sponsor, he had about 25 component sponsors that included, Lunati Cams, Carrera Shocks, Flex-A-Foam, C.J. Rayburn Race Cars, and long time sponsor Winters Performance Products, willing to help fund the series.

Robert said that even with the Stroh's sponsorship he had sunk over $80,000 of his own money into the series in '85. He claims he canceled the Stroh's contract for '86 because of a $5 million dollar insurance requirement that he simply could not afford. Smawley said the 1986 season could have happened, but the shows would have been with less fanfare, no high dollar advertising budgets, and a smaller driver points fund. In an article released before the '86 NDRA season, Robert had already moved into bigger offices, and had even released a 20 race schedule for the upcoming season. In addition, he was actively looking for a national sponsor. I don't think a downsized NDRA is what Robert Smawley envisioned as the future of his "Traveling Dirt Show." According to Buddy Duke and others close to Robert, "He wanted to play big or not at all."

The NDRA vs. STARS rivalry is often mentioned as another reason why Robert Smawley pulled the plug on his series. The Short Track Auto Racing Series (STARS) was organized after the 1983 racing season by Carl Short at the half-mile Pennsboro (WV) Speedway; Frank Plessinger at the Hagerstown (MD) Speedway; and Satch Worley at Log Cabin (VA) Raceway. The three race track promoters planned to

STARS Changes Hands: Schedule Out

PARKERSBURG, WV — The Short Track Auto Racing Series (STARS), started two years ago by Pennsboro Speedway's Carl Short to promote special events at dirt tracks throughout the United States, has been sold to a group of three promoters who have hosted STARS events.

Dave Ashley, promotional director at West Virginia Motor Speedway in Parkersburg; Don Gross, owner of Buckeye Speedway in Orrville, OH; and Roger Williams of Brownstown (IN) Speedway have purchased the STARS organization and will run a complete 1986 schedule.

Ashley, president of the new group, said STARS would now stand for Short Track Auto Racing Stars with the group incorporated as such in Ohio. Gross will be secretary-treasurer and Williams vice president.

Short decided to sell the organization due to the serious illness of his father in South Carolina and his father's need for constant care.

Seventeen events are listed on the 1986 STARS schedule, beginning with a two event weekend in Tennessee the last weekend in April. A complete schedule will be released soon.

Ashley said drivers and fans won't find many changes other than a change in the top brass with most tracks hosting past events doing so again.

At this time, STARS is not offering a points fund but will continue to offer high-paying minimum purses for each event. Ashley feels drivers are bettered served by high paying races throughout the season rather than sacrificing the individual race purse structure for a point fund.

However, Ashley said the new STARS is pursuing new sponsors for future point fund monies and contingency awards.

The temporary STARS phone number is (614) 423-6758.

Short Track Auto Racing Stars (STARS) 1986 Schedule

Date	Event	Track	Location
Apr. 25,26	Pepsi-Cola 100	Winchester Speedway	Winchester, TN
May 17	Kenny Simpson Memorial	Brownstown Speedway	Brownstown, IN
May 18		Tri-State Speedway	Haubstadt, IN
May 31	Alpine-Alpa 100	Buckeye Speedway	Orrville, OH
Jun. 8	Special Olympics 100	West Virginia Motor Speedway	Mineral Wells, WV
Jun. 27		Bloomington Speedway	Bloomington, IN
Jun. 28	Hoosier Dirt Classic	Brownstown Speedway	Brownstown, IN
Aug. 3	Shrine National Championship	West Virginia Motor Speedway	Mineral Wells, WV
Aug. 8,9	Rebel 100 Classic	Winchester Speedway	Winchester, TN
Aug. 16	Jackson 100	Brownstown Speedway	Brownstown, IN
Aug. 17		Tri-State Speedway	Haubstadt, IN
Aug. 29		Muskingum County Speedway	Zanesville, OH
Aug. 30	Buckeye Nationals	Buckeye Speedway	Orrville, OH
Aug. 31	Hillbilly 100	Pennsboro Speedway	Pennsboro, WV
Oct. 18,19	Dirt Track World Championship	Pennsboro Speedway	Pennsboro, WV

July and September Dates To Be Announced

---

run events in the East and Midwest in 1984. Most of their races were held in Virginia, Maryland, Indiana, West Virginia, Ohio, and one race in North Carolina in the inaugural '84 season. The '85 season saw the STARS series run 29 races, including the first five at Volusia County (FLA) Speedway in February. Again, most of their races, after the February races, were held in the same states as the '84 season, with the exception of one race in Kentucky, and three races in Pennsylvania.

Carl Short was the man responsible for taking Eldora Speedways, Earl Baltes big money purses to the next level, with the $30,000 to win races he started handing out at his Famed Pennsboro Speedway. In 1981 Jim Dunn won the first Dirt Track World Championship and the $30,000 winner's share that went with it. Short told me at the 2015

The Rock-em, Sock-em, Travelin' Sideways Dirt Show

DTWC, "This was twice as much as had ever been paid out for a dirt at that time." Short said he arrived at that figure, "Because that was what The Southern 500 at Darlington was paying to win that year."

As far as the rivalry goes, both Smawley and Short accused the other of telling mistruths and spreading rumors. As a result, a bitter racing purse war started, with one trying to "out dollar" the other. Robert said, "If I had a race paying $10,000, Carl would have one at the same time paying $20,000." This went on for a while according to Rodney Combs, "It split the drivers and fans up. At one time the NDRA had the best dirt drivers in the world. It was as simple as that."

Smawley ran most of his races during "84 and "85 in the South, with a few races in Missouri, Arkansas, and Kansas. There was an '85 race at Auto City Speedway in Flint, Michigan. The only races Robert held in STARS territory was a race in 1984 at TriState Speedway at Haubstadt, Indiana, the Flint Race mentioned above, and a race at West Virginia Motor speedway in Mineral Wells, West Virginia in '85. As you can see, the two series were basically in two different parts of the country.

Both series ended at about the same time, Smawley ended his NDRA series after the '85 season. At the end of the '85 season, Carl Short sold his STARS series to another group of promoters that included, Dave Ashley of West Virginia Motor Speedway; Don Gross of Buckeye Speedway; and Roger Williams of Brownstown Speedway. This Group ran a new STARS series, beginning with the 1986 season.

The NDRA had the national sponsors with a high prospect of maintaining a national sponsor for the '86 season. On the other hand, STARS had several component sponsors like Malcuit Racing Engines and no major national sponsor on the level of the NDRA's, Consolidated Cigar Corporation (Dutch Treats), or the Chrysler Corporation. Smawley said, "If the NDRA was left alone, if other promoters didn't try to compete with it and copy it, the NDRA would still be around."

Maybe, if both series would have worked together, like today's Lucas Oil Late Model Dirt Series and the World of Outlaws Late Model Series, both could have survived and found their own niche in the world of late model dirt racing. The Lucas series operates mainly in the South, while the World of Outlaws runs mainly in the Northern states. This is very similar what STARS and the NDRA were doing at the time. As they say in football, "Maybe a little less trash talk would have been good for both these promoters and their series'."

At times the STARS vs. NDRA was a bitter rivalry. However, according Buddy and Cotton Duke and others who were close to Smawley, it was not what caused Robert to suddenly end his national dirt series. After talking to Buddy and Cotton Duke, Doug Sopha, and many others familiar with Smawley and his series, I also think this rivalry had very little to do with the demise of the NDRA.

So, if it wasn't the STARS vs. NDRA rivalry or one of the other reasons mentioned above, what did cause the sudden end the Robert's, "Traveling Dirt Show?" We will look at what caused Smawley to suddenly pull the plug on his series after the 1985 season, leaving both drivers and race fans to wonder what happened. Thirty year later, it is still a mystery to many in the dirt racing world.

Chapter Ten

The End of the Dream - Why Robert Pulled the Plug

It all started as a dream – a vision in the mind of perhaps the most colorful promoter dirt track racing will ever see. A Kingsport, Tennessee promoter by the name of Robert Wayne Smawley was hell bent on making a late model dirt version of Bill France's NASCAR. In the end, it became much more than he could possible handle. However, through the pages of this book, you became witness to how Robert came so damn close to making his, "Rock-Em, Sock-em, Travelin' Sideways Dirt Show," a reality.

Make no mistake, Smawley was a showman, a promoter, and a visionary thinker who clearly changed the sport of late model dirt racing forever. Beginning with his first "test race" at Newport, Tennessee in June of 1978, all of dirt racing, from the drivers, to the fans, to the track owners and promoters; and even the news media, knew they were witnessing a historic change in the dirt track racing world. They saw a different type of dirt racing show. For example, there were the unheard of (at the time) $10,000 to win purses; the new promotional ideas (such as having local businesses involved with the races) and having contingency awards for the drivers (like the $10,000 Dutch Treats fast qualifier award); the colorful pageantry of the races (having rousing renditions of "Dixie" played at a lot of the Southern tracks); and the national sponsorships, like Schlitz, Stroh's, Consolidated Cigar Corporation, and the Chrysler Corporation. These corporate sponsors helped usher in a national following, and provided money for large series points funds, and the ever increasing racing purses. Robert brought all these new ideas and more to dirt racing in the almost eight year run of the NDRA.

Those closest to Robert, like Buddy and Cotton Duke, Bill Dale, Johnny Robinson, Doug Sopha, Jo Zimmerman, Eva Taylor, Connie Noel, and others, knew in the beginning that Robert had a hands on approach to everything he did. He wanted to be involved in every aspect of his series. Robert wanted to do the planning, promoting, advertising, organizing the drivers, and making national race fans out of

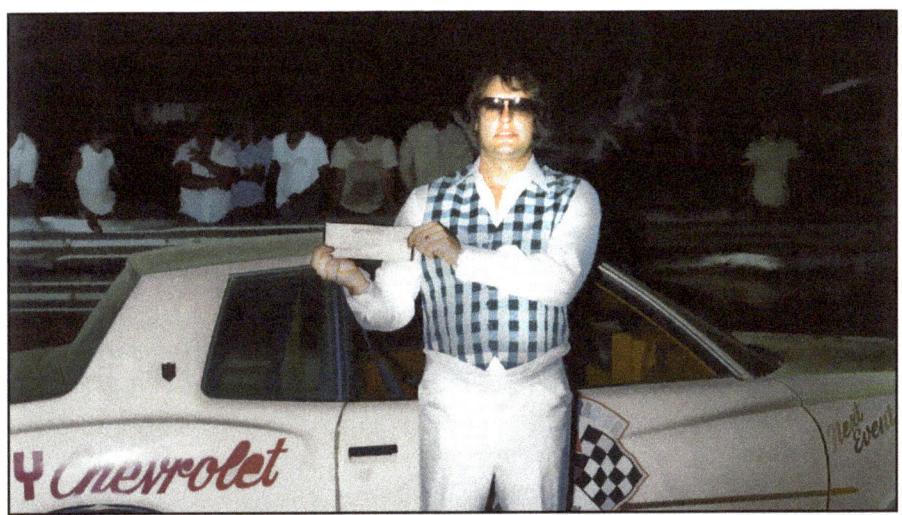

Robert holding one of his famous $10,000 to win checks. Photo from the Robert Smawley collection.

regional fans. In other words, he basically wanted to do "everything himself." Buddy Duke recently told me, "He would come to me and assign me three or four things to do, but most times before I could get started, he would already have everything he had assigned to me done." Buddy went on to say, "I'd ask him why he did the things I was supposed to do, and he'd say, I just wanted to help." Duke concluded by saying, "This was just the way Robert was, he wanted to try and do everything pertaining to the series himself."

In the beginning, Smawley wanted to run a race every week. This went on for a while, until he saw it would be pretty much impossible to maintain that kind of pace. This was evidenced in a classic Smawley quote in an interview once. He said, "If you're on the ball, promoting can cut 15 to 20 years off your life." This could have been especially true as the series grew, 28 races (a series high) in '81, and 24 races in '82.

There was no one "magical" reason that ended the NDRA. It was a combination of a number of reasons all rolled into one. Over and over, this is what I continued to hear from the people who were the closest to Robert Smawley.

Most of those reasons were discussed in the last chapter and no further mention is needed here. One must keep in mind, Smawley was a complex person who had a unique ability to think "outside the

The Rock-em, Sock-em, Travelin' Sideways Dirt Show

box," before it was vogue to do so. As we have seen, many of his ideas were simply years ahead of their time. For example, his wanting to record every aspect of his dirt series was a clear illustration of "reality" television long before its time.

Because of his unique personality, he wanted to have his hands in all areas of the series. Robert wanted to be the organizer, series president, marketing director, promoter, driver recruiter, master of ceremonies, the race fans best friend, and the list just kept growing. The series itself kept getting bigger and bigger, like a snowball going downhill. Meanwhile, Robert got closer and closer to taking his "dirt version" of NASCAR from a dream to a reality. Then one day it became too much for even the "king of all racing promoters," to handle by himself. His failure to put his trust in others, is what I and many others believe caused the demise of the National Dirt Racing Association. The series had simply become too big and too complex to be a one man show any longer. Finally, as we saw in the last chapter, the stress of trying to make it a one man show became just too much in the end.

Add to that a little known fact to many in the racing world; during the last few years of the NDRA, Smawley was diagnosed with congestive heart disease. In a recent interview with long time friend Buddy Duke, he said, "Robert was actually hospitalized for a time during the NDRA series for heart problems." Buddy said, "After that last race in '85, Robert said to me as we left the track that night, 'Buddy I have just had enough of this damn series and all its problems. That's it!'"

Robert Wayne Smawley died of Leukemia on October 1, 1998. After his death he was given late model dirt racing's ultimate honor in 2001, when he was inducted into the National Dirt Late Model Hall of Fame as a hall of fame promoter. Like him or not, late model dirt racing owes him credit for organizing the first national touring series for dirt late models. He took dirt racing from a regional sport, to the national dirt racing scene, professionalizing the sport and its drivers along the way.

The Lucas Oil Late Model Dirt Series and the World of Outlaws Late Model Series are here today as a result of Robert and his, "Rock-Em, Sock-Em, Travelin' Sideways Dirt Show." The series that will always be known to the racing world as Robert Smawley's NDRA.

Gary L. Parker

More Photos from the Rock-em, Sock-em, Travelin' Sideways Dirt Show

#1- Bobby Thomas with Jo Zimmerman (in hat), he won the first official NDRA race held at East Alabama Motor Speedway (photo by Al Eaves)

#2- A couple of Schlitz Pro-National drivers taking a break at an NDRA race (photo from the Robert Smawley collection).

#3- Billy Thomas, Buck Simmons, and Bobby Thomas enjoying a laugh between heat races at Phenix City, Alabama (the Robert Smawley collection).

#4- Billy Thomas and Robert Smawley at a Reed Cams Race (photo from the Robert Smawley collection).

#5- Tom Helfrich enjoying the spoils of victory (photo by David Chobat).

#6- A recent photo of me [Gary parker, the author] and former NDRA flagman, Bob Smith. (photo taken at the 2015 DTWC).

#7- Larry Moore enjoys a victory kiss after a Schlitz Pro-National win. Notice the fender skirt on his car, NICE (photo from the Robert Smawley collection).

#8- The ever showman, Robert Smawley as Georgia driver Stan Massey looks on with a laugh (photo from the Robert Smawley collection).

#9- Buck Simmons, Kenny McCurry, Miss NDRA Eva Taylor (WOW), and Robert Smawley enjoy a fun moment before a race at Rome (GA) Speedway (photo from the Robert Smawley collection).

#10-Rodney Combs celebrating a victory with trophy queens and Robert. Wonder why Rodney is smiling? (photo by David Chobat).

#11- Charlie Mincey and his wife enjoy a celebration with Robert before receiving a trophy (photo from the Robert Smawley collection).

#12- Robert Surrounded by some of his many beautiful Trophy girls (photo from the Robert Smawley collection).

#13- More of Robert's trophy girls. I knew you wouldn't mind seeing more of these beauties (photo from the Robert Smawley collection).

#14- How about a few more (photo from the Robert Smawley collection).

#15- Georgia's Doug Kenimer after an NDRA win receiving a trophy from Robert and the beautiful trophy queens (photo from the Robert Smawley collection).

#16- The Schlitz Malt Liquor Bull giving some last minute race advice to Kentucky driver Jack Boggs (photo from the Robert Smawley collection).

#17- Robert with National Speed Sport's, Chris Economaki (photo from the Robert Smawley collection).

#18- The ever colorful Smawley enjoying a chat before an NDRA race (photo by David Chobat).

#19- The Schlitz Pro-National show van (photo fro the Robert Smawley collection).

#20- The Schlitz Pro-National Corvette NDRA dirt car (photo from the Robert Smawley collection).

#21- The Schlitz Pro-National van and race car (photo from the Robert Smawley collection).

#22- NDRA driver, Jerry Inmon (#D-7) in action (photo from the Robert Smawley collection).

#23- Driver C.L. Pritchett powers through a turn at Anderson(SC) Speedway in 1979. Note the Pepsi NDRA sanctioned sign in the background (photo provided by Larry Mazza, a great dirt race fan).

#24- Washington Georgia's, Roscoe Smith #44 (photo by David Chobat).

#25- Fulmer Lance #21 and Buck Simmons #41 on the pole for an NDRA race (photo from the Robert Smawley collection).

The Rock-em, Sock-em, Travelin' Sideways Dirt Show

#26- 1979 NDRA Champion, Leon Archer #222 passes a lapped car on his way to a win (photo by David Chobat).

#27 Roseville, Ohio's Jim Dunn hot lapping during an NDRA race in his signature D-1 DIRT race car (photo by David Chobat).

#28- Jim Dunn qualifying for an NDRA race (photo by David Chobat).

#29- Florida driver Dick Anderson stand beside his Bopp Chassis #92 (photo by David Chobat).

#30- Plainville, Indiana driver Buck Ridenour hot laps in the #11 Moe's Body Shop race car (photo by David Chobat).

#31- Jim Curry of Norman, Indiana qualifying for an NDRA race (photo by David Chobat).

#32- Three wide out of turn four at the Pontiac Silverdome (photo from the Robert Smawley collection).

#33- Jack Boggs #B4 battles the Flintstone Flyer Mike Duvall during the Silverdome race (photo from the Robert Smawley collection).

#34- An overflow crowd for an NDRA race at the famed Atomic (TN) Speedway (photo from the Robert Smawley collection).

#35- There were always plenty of pretty girls and hoopla after an NDRA win. Here Leon Archer appears to be a bit overwhelmed with it all after his NDRA win at Myrtle Beach (photo by David Chobat).

#36- The official NDRA scorekeepers, Chris and Brenda Boals (photo provided by Betty Vineyard-Price).

#37- Darwin "Shon" Price sold official NDRA souvenirs (photo provided by Betty Vineyard-Price).

#38- Betty Vineyard-Price sold official NDRA souvenirs and kept up with the kids (photo provided by Betty Vineyard-Price).

#39- Betty and Shon's children, Marty, Jason, and Lori, along with Doug Sopha's son, Christopher (photo provided by Betty Vineyard-Price).

#40- Young Jason and Marty looking over some of the NDRA hats (photo provided by Betty Vineyard-Price).

#41- Hoosier Tire Rep and friend of Robert, Doug Sopha (photo provided by Betty Vineyard-Price).

The Rock-em, Sock-em, Travelin' Sideways Dirt Show

#42- This is Betty, Fred, and Shon at an NDRA race in the Midwest before the souvenir trailer (photo provided by Betty Vineyard-Price).

#43- The official NDRA souvenir truck and trailer (photo provided by Betty Vineyard-Price).

#44- The souvenir trailer "open for business" (photo provided by Betty Vineyard-Price).

#45- The Stroh's show car, van and race car (photo provided by Betty Vineyard-Price).

#46- Jim Dunn powers out of a turn in the famous DIRT late model race car (photo provided by Betty Vineyard-Price).

#47- Freddy Smith and Jeff Purvis take a moment before the start of a race in the Midwest, one of the many flat tracks found there (photo provided by Betty Vineyard-Price).

#48- NDRA star Larry Moore's #M14 race car loaded on his van and trailer (photo provided by Betty Vineyard-Price).

#49- Larry Moore stands beside his #14 race car (photo provided by Betty Vineyard-Price).

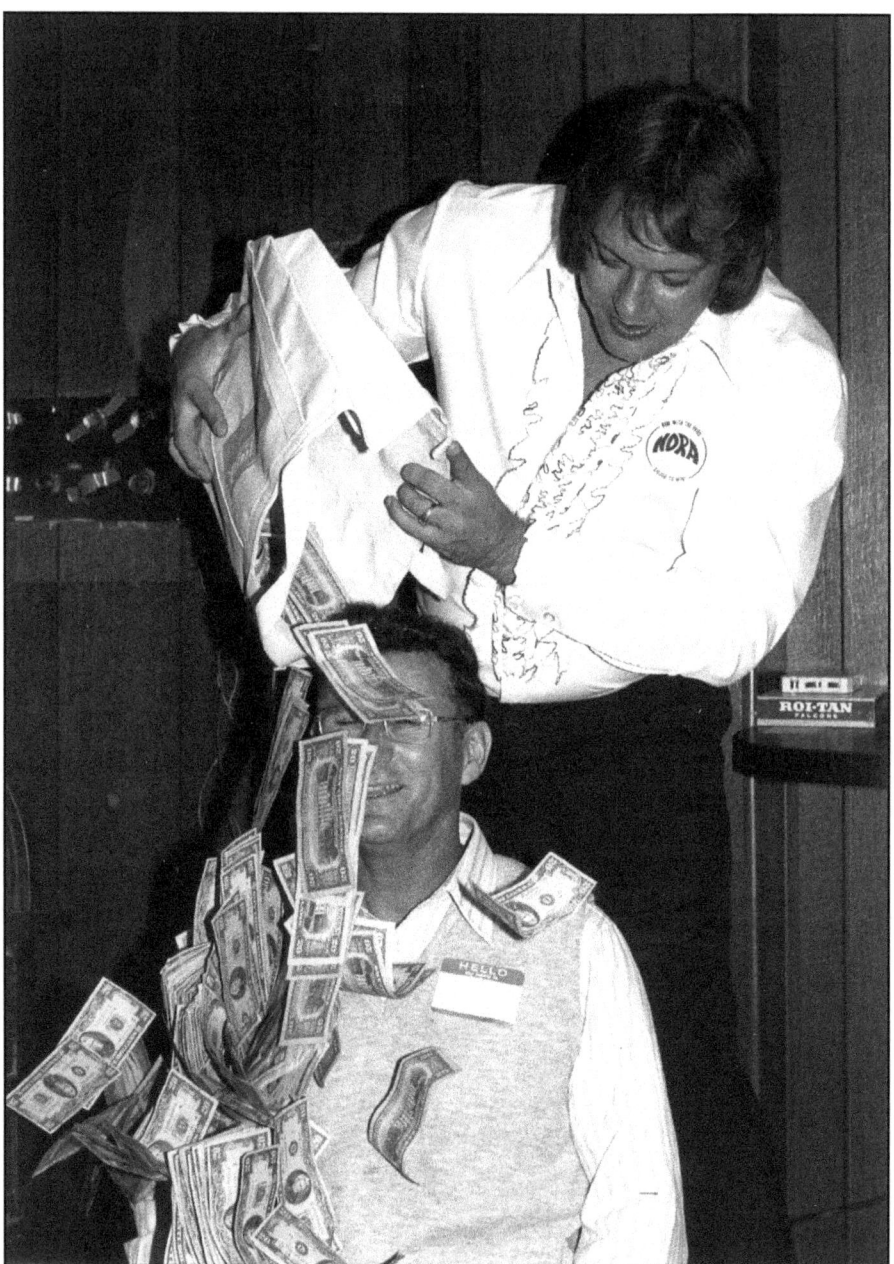

#50- Finally, say what you will, Smawley brought money and fame to dirt racing. He brought dirt racing to where it is today. Along the way, he professionalized the drivers and made late model dirt racing into a national sport. Thanks Robert, "This Stroh's Is For You."

To order more copies of
The Rock-em, Sock-em, Travelin' Sideways Dirt Show

Copy this page, complete information, and mail with check or money order to address below

Name _____

Shipping address _____

City_____ State_____ Zip_____

Phone_____ E-mail (optional for shipping confirmation) _____

    Quantity _____ book(s) @ $24.95   = $ _____
    Shipping first book   = $ __5.00__
    Shipping quantity _____ additional books @ $3.00   = $ _____
    TN residents add sales tax @ .0925   = $ _____
                                    TOTAL   = $ _____

To order more copies of
Red Clay and Dust

Copy this page, complete information, and mail with check or money order to adress below

Name _____

Shipping address _____

City_____ State_____ Zip_____

Phone_____ E-mail (optional for shipping confirmation) _____

    Quantity _____ book(s) @ $24.95   = $ _____
    Shipping first book   = $ __5.00__
    Shipping quantity _____ additional books @ $3.00   = $ _____
    TN residents add sales tax @ .0925   = $ _____
                                    TOTAL   = $ _____

Mail completed form with check or money order to:
Gary Parker, 1517 Maxwell Road, Chattanooga, TN 37412
423-580-2690 • eparker0923@gmail.com • or go to
www.waldenhouse.com – or – www.amazon.com

Myriad Pro and Comic Sans on LSI 70# white
Type and design by Karen Paul Stone

www.ingramcontent.com/pod-product-compliance
Lightning Source LLC
Chambersburg PA
CBHW041952180426
43199CB00038B/2889